UNIVERSITY COLLEGE BIRMINGHAM
COLLEGE LIBRARY, SUMMER ROW
BIRMINGHAM. B3 1JB
Tel: (0121) 243 0055

DATE OF RETURN

5 OCT 2009		

Please remember to return on time or pay the fine

The Kogan Page Practical Trainer Series

Series Editor: Roger Buckley

PRACTICAL TRAINER SERIES

KOGAN PAGE

How to Take a Training Audit

MICHAEL APPLEGARTH

KOGAN PAGE
Published in association with the
Institute of Training and Development

First published in 1991
Reprinted 1992, 1993

Kogan Page Limited
120 Pentonville Road
London N1 9JN

British Library Cataloguing in Publication Data

A CIP record for this book is available from the British Library.

ISBN 07494 0429 9

Typeset by Saxon Printing Ltd, Derby
Printed and bound in Great Britain by
Biddles Ltd, Guildford and King's Lynn

Contents

Series Editor's Foreword

Organizations get things done when people do their jobs effectively. To make this happen they need to be well trained. A number of people are likely to be involved in this training by identifying the needs of the organization and of the individual, by selecting or designing appropriate training to meet those needs, by delivering it and by assessing how effective it was. It is not only 'professional' or full-time trainers who are involved in this process; personnel managers, line managers, supervisors and job holders are all likely to have a part to play.

This series has been written for all those who get involved with training in some way or another, whether they are senior personnel managers trying to link the goals of the organization with training needs or job holders who have been given responsibility for training newcomers. Therefore, the series is essentially a practical one which focuses on specific aspects of the training function. This is not to say that the theoretical underpinnings of the practical aspects of training are unimportant. Anyone seriously interested in training is strongly encouraged to look beyond 'what to do' and 'how to do it' and to delve into the areas of why things are done in a particular way.

The authors have been selected because they have considerable practical experience. All have shared, at some time, the same difficulties, frustrations and satisfactions of being involved in training and are now in a position to share with others some helpful and practical guidelines.

In this book, Michael Applegarth shows how trainers can provide an answer to the question: 'Is our training worth the money we are spending on it?' It is frustrating when the benefits of training cannot be costed with accuracy. The Training Audit is a method of assessing, in non-financial terms, the value that an organization can place on its training. This kind of audit should not be confused with the validation which forms part of the training cycle; it plays more of an inspectorial role to ensure that validation is being done properly. In the same way, the Training Audit examines all stages of the training cycle and should be regarded as a superordinate function which monitors and regulates training to ensure that the organization gets value for money.

ROGER BUCKLEY

Acknowledgements

I take this opportunity to acknowledge gratefully the support, co-operation and contributions made by the following:

The National Audit Office, for providing valuable background and research material.

London and Edinburgh Insurance Group, for allowing me to reproduce the Training and Development Progression Plan shown in the case study at the end of Chapter 4.

Reliance Security Services, for consenting to share with us the case study at the end of Chapter 5.

Godfrey Durham Training Consultants Ltd, not only for permitting me to reproduce extracts from the Learning Agreement, but also for the encouragement given by the Managing Director and colleagues.

The TEED, for its consent to the reproduction of extracts from the National Standards for Training & Development (developed by the TDLB), and the Management Charter Initiative, for its permission to reproduce the framework for Module I of its Occupational Standards for Managers.

Prologue

Once Upon a Time ... Well Almost!

Imagine the following meeting taking place in a managing director's office, somewhere. Three managers are present.

The MD begins: 'Times are hard, I've got to shed some overheads. Tell me why I should keep each of you employed.'

The production manager replies first. She says: 'My role contributes to the revenue of the company, rather than costs the company.'

'Why's that?' asks the MD.

'Well, in the last two years, I've streamlined the production process so that it now costs us 50 per cent less in real terms to produce 1,000 units.

Every 1,000 units produced and sold is equivalent to 10 per cent of my salary. We still need a product to sell and usually we sell 2,000 units per month. So after five months, I've contributed to the cost of my salary. That means that seven months of the year is clear profit to the company. So if I'm making you money, why get rid of me?'

The MD presses a few buttons on his musical calculator and beams impressively at the production manager. 'OK', he says, 'you can stay.'

He then turns to the marketing manager, who defends himself by saying: 'I too can bring in revenue rather than consume costs.'

'Tell me more,' says the MD.

'Well, as you know, there are many other companies producing products similar to ours. We will lose money when we produce units but can't attract customers to them.

My role is to show those who need the product that ours is the best for them, and to show those who don't know such a product exists that they need our units too.

Every £100 I spend on marketing returns us £500 within a month. So if I spend £1,000 per month we can draw in about £5,000 per month. Well, that's twice as much as I earn, so I represent 50 per cent profit to the company.'

The MD again looks impressed, and so allows the third person a chance to make his case. He invites the training manager to speak.

The training manager replies: 'I always get good feedback from my courses and everyone enjoys them. It's obvious, if they enjoy themselves, they'll work harder!'

The MD, the production manager and the marketing manager now all look expectantly at the training manager. After a minute he says: 'Goodbye!'

Perhaps this is a rather far-fetched and slightly glib account of a company's dilemma – but one that during a recession (as experienced in the latter part of 1990 and early 1991) has possibly been enacted, not verbatim of course, in hundreds of board rooms.

In fact, it might be more real to suggest that the decision to dispense with the training department will already have been made, without the training manager having had the opportunity to make a case for his or her defence.

Introduction

Value-for-Money Audits

If only the training carried out in companies could speak for itself and be recognized, at board level and below, as a contribution to saving money. To dispense with training altogether, as a cost-cutting exercise, can be suicidal: to diminish its resources to the equivalent of a 'token' trainer with £100 to spend, is most likely to prove a false economy. Economy is a word that occurs again and again during troubled times, yet survival is not merely a matter of making economies.

In Chapter 2 we see what is involved in a 'training audit', but it may be helpful to recognize what auditing, itself, is all about. In its simplest terms an audit is an investigation of current practice against 'best practice'. It is a way of identifying the practice and procedures in operation and exploring whether or not they achieve the desired outcome. In doing this, however, the question also being asked is, 'Can it be done better?' If economy is called into question along with efficiency and effectiveness, the result becomes a value for money (VFM) audit.

The professionals in conducting VFM audits are the National Audit Office (NAO) in the UK, and its equivalent in the USA, the General Accounting Office (GAO). The primary role of the NAO is 'to provide independent assurance, information and advice to Parliament on the accounts of government departments and a wide range of public bodies, and on the economy, efficiency and effectiveness with which they use their resources.' (Extracted from the *Annual Report* of the NAO, 1990.)

Good trainers always learn from the professionals. This book is no exception, in that it does not try to re-invent the wheel but it does design the wheel to conform to the vehicle which it supports. During my research, it was reassuring to discover that the proposed training audit path was in line with the NAO's own approach to value for money audits. Yet in answering the question: 'Why bother with a training audit?' we can draw on their experience and on the findings of a survey they carried out in 1988–9 in the UK, comparing the training of non-industrial civil servants (public sector employees) with training in the private sector.

Whether your company is large or small, and whether it has an established training function or not, the practices discussed in this book should be compared to your own to see where improvements could be made.

Perhaps you don't have a training function as yet: in which case you can get a head start without bad habits blocking your way. The following chapters are as much about establishing a training function from scratch as they are about auditing what is already there.

1 Why Bother with a Training Audit?

▷ ## SUMMARY ◁

- Explains why we should bother with a training audit. While the Introduction told us something about value-for-money audits, here we define the contributions of economy, efficiency and effectiveness.
- Describes quality standards and competence-based performance standards, both of which make the task of auditing training that much easier.
- Discounts a cost-benefit analysis as an outcome of the training audit, before reviewing the findings of a National Audit Office report and its implications for the training auditor.

Doing it with Es

One thing immediately evident from the National Audit Office's own definition of its role ('to provide independent assurance, information and advice to Parliament on the accounts of government departments and a wide range of public bodies, and on the economy, efficiency and effectiveness with which they use their resources'), is that it never looks at economy in isolation. In fact, it identifies three elements of value for money:

- Economy.
- Efficiency.
- Effectiveness.

The NAO's own definition of each is:

Economy is concerned with minimizing the cost of resources acquired or used, having regard to quality.

Efficiency is concerned with the relationship between the output of goods, services or other results and the resources used to produce them. How far is maximum output achieved for a given input, or minimum input used for a given output?

Effectiveness is concerned with the relationship between the intended results and the actual results of projects, programmes or other activities. How successfully do output of goods, services or other results achieve policy objectives, operational goals and other intended effects?

In short they can be expressed as:

- Spending less.
- Spending well.
- Spending wisely.

Even the professionals acknowledge that the distinctions between each are not always clear-cut. The ultimate measure, though, at the end of any audit is not whether a project, programme or department is economical, but whether it is effective.

Effectiveness

Within the definition of effectiveness, given earlier, was the suggestion of objectives being achieved. What this in turn implies is that the degree of effectiveness is derived from the use of performance measures and indicators.

The training profession has been helped recently with the advent of quality standards and competence-based performance standards. Each has the effect of giving yardsticks by which performance, and hence effectiveness, are assessed. To many of us, they may be no more than common sense under new labels. Yet if common sense and good practice are the same, this is what an audit likes to see operating.

Quality standards

Many manufacturing concerns, in particular, are presently trying to get to grips with quality standards. Essentially, these are quality systems' specifications for design, development, production, installation and servicing, which can be applied to a company's activities. Within each specification is the requirement that training is approached systematically rather than haphazardly; therefore standards cannot be achieved without such compliance from training.

In the UK the relevant standard is referred to as BS 5750, Part 1, 1987; the equivalent in the United States is ISO 9001, 1987; while in

Europe it is recognized as EN 29001, 1987. Attainment of one of these standards is a valuable indicator to customers that the product or service will consistently meet its specified requirements.

Competence-based performance standards

Competence-based performance standards, on the other hand, are recent innovations on both sides of the Atlantic. However, the concept of the USA version regards *competencies* as attributes of an individual, whereas in the UK *competences* are regarded as outcomes, or employer expectation, of workplace performance.

In the UK, generic standards are being set across the spectrum of industry by Industry Lead Bodies (ILBs) who set out the task requirements of particular occupations or job roles. In the USA, a generic competency model has been developed by McBer and Company for the American Management Association, yet it is very different from the UK approach. It identifies behaviours which are characteristic of superior-performing managers across a variety of sectors and jobs. These behaviours are grouped into 18 competencies, which in turn are grouped under four clusters:

1. Goal and action management.
2. Directing subordinates.
3. Human resources management.
4. Leadership.

Contrast this, however, with Figure 1.1, showing the occupational standards for managers developed in the UK by the Management Charter Initiative (MCI). While there is no uniformity of style between the two, they still contribute towards a 'best-practice' approach.

If companies are presently trying to get to grips with these standards, does that mean then, that common sense and good practice were perhaps not common after all?

There lies the purpose and outcome of a training audit. The practice we apply may be performed well, but what are we not applying that could enhance our performance and virtually guarantee a quality product or service? That is the difference between efficiency and effectiveness.

Efficiency	*Effectiveness*
Doing a thing the right way.	Doing the right thing the right way.

Effectiveness should also consider the value of the objectives set. You can only know you are doing the right thing if you know what your purpose is. Yet, if that purpose is of little value to your employer,

Key purpose: To achieve the organization's objectives and continuously improve its performance

Units of Competence and their associated Elements of Competence

UNITS	ELEMENTS

I 1 Maintain and improve service and product operations	1.1 Maintain operations to meet quality standards
	1.2 Create and maintain the necessary conditions for productive work
I 2 Contribute to the implementation of change in services, products and systems	2.1 Contribute to the evaluation of proposed changes to services, products and systems
	2.2 Implement and evaluate changes to services, products and systems
I 3 Recommend, monitor and control the use of resources	3.1 Make recommendations for expenditure
	3.2 Monitor and control the use of resources
I 4 Contribute to the recruitment and selection of personnel	4.1 Define future personnel requirements
	4.2 Contribute to the assessment and selection of candidates against team and organisational requirements
I 5 Develop teams, individuals and self to enhance performance	5.1 Develop and improve teams through planning and activities
	5.2 Identify, review and improve development activities for individuals
	5.3 Develop oneself within the job role
I 6 Plan, allocate and evaluate work carried out by teams, individuals and self	6.1 Set and update work objectives for teams and individuals
	6.2 Plan activities and determine work methods to achieve objectives
	6.3 Allocate work and evaluate teams, individuals and self against objectives
	6.4 Provide feedback to teams and individuals on their performance
I 7 Create, maintain and enhance effective working relationships	7.1 Establish and maintain the trust and support of one's subordinates
	7.2 Establish and maintain the trust and support of one's immediate manager
	7.3 Establish and maintain relationships with colleagues
	7.4 Identify and minimise interpersonal conflict
	7.5 Implement disciplinary and grievance procedures
	7.6 Counsel staff
I 8 Seek, evaluate and organise information for action	8.1 Obtain and evaluate information to aid decision making
	8.2 Record and store information
I 9 Exchange information to solve problems and make decisions	9.1 Lead meetings and group discussions to solve problems and make decisions
	9.2 Contribute to discussions to solve problems and make decisions
	9.3 Advise and inform others

effectiveness in the job that you have may not be enough to avoid the hatchet.

The Training Auditor

Unlike the National Audit Office, or General Accounting Office, it is most unlikely that the training auditor will be independent or uninvolved in the training function being audited – unless an external training consultant is called in. More usually, the training manager may be the auditor too. This may create problems of objectivity, but if the manager applies the procedures highlighted in the following chapters, he or she will still be able to find ways of maximizing value for money and identifying actions needed to improve practice and procedures.

In particular, the training auditor needs to review whether the training function is:

- Working towards valued objectives.
- Applying sound and efficient procedures.
- Obtaining the appropriate type, quality and quantity of resources when needed, at the lowest cost.
- Avoiding duplication of effort and work that serves little or no purpose.
- Complying with any laws and regulations affecting the company.
- Equipped to provide information on the economy, efficiency and effectiveness of training.

The role will certainly require a thorough understanding of the organization, its policies and objectives, procedures and controls, main activities and available resources.

As a non-independent party it is appropriate, in this case, that the auditor questions the value of objectives, as proposed above. The NAO, on the other hand, would take the objectives for granted and comment on the extent to which they have been achieved. This avoids accusations that they are questioning policy, whereas, as we shall see in Chapter 2, the first stage of the training audit is to question the training policy.

Value for Money v. Cost-benefit Analysis

To refer to some further NAO terminology: when we are concerned with the effectiveness of training we are concerned with the *impact* that training has on the organization. If we are looking at value-for-money judgements, then perhaps we should look at impacts in cash terms. We can then compare the money put into training (investment) with the monetary value of the impact (return).

Unfortunately, even value-for-money audits cannot be that precise. While we can accurately assess training costs, it is not always possible to put true cash values on the outcome of training. What cash return could you attach to the impact that a one-week's management development programme has had on a line manager? When will the impact be evident: within one week, one month, or in a year's time?

Furthermore, in assessing the impact of training on performance, how can we be certain that the improvement in performance was the direct result of the training, and not the result of better motivation or rewards, or an improvement in personal circumstances?

But don't despair; even if we cannot calculate a cash value for the impact of the training, we can still assess whether:

- The objectives were correctly set.
- The objectives were achieved.
- Performance of the trainee has improved, and to the extent required.

We can also calculate the cost of the training and thereby arrive at a measure of its cost-effectiveness, or value for money. This is not the same as a cost-benefit analysis, which would put money values on the benefits or outcomes of training, but it is the nearest we can get to assessing the effectiveness of training within the business environment.

Results of the National Audit Office Report

It is worth noting the opening paragraph to the NAO report, referred to earlier, on the *Training of Non-Industrial Civil Servants*. It reads:

Training is investment in people. Its purpose is to increase staff competence and develop staff potential, and, thereby, to improve organisational performance. It is as important to an organisation as sound capital investment and deserves equally careful attention.

That last sentence reiterates the importance of the training audit.

Some of the findings and conclusions of the Report give us a good clue as to the issues which may surface when conducting our own training audits:

Civil Service
1. In 1988–9 non-industrial civil servants spent an average of 4.1 days each on training.
2. Junior and middle managers received the most training.
3. Responsibility for identifying individual needs was firmly placed on the immediate line manager during annual staff reporting procedures.
4. Each department examined had some form of overall planning and performance review system, though there were no systematic arrangements for identifying and aggregating the training needs that resulted, or for prioritizing them.
5. Individual courses were generally relevant to departments' needs and competently and effectively delivered. But central co-ordination was variable and there were weaknesses in the quantification of objectives and the appraisal of training investment.
6. The quality of data produced for measuring the impact of training was very variable. Performance against objectives was assessed, but not systematically; evaluation of the benefits of training was at an early stage.
7. There were often no systematic arrangements for confirming that priority needs were being met, for exploring options for the delivery of training, or for investigating the balance of costs and benefits envisaged from the investment involved.
8. The extent to which actual data on training costs was available depended partly on departments' budgeting arrangements. In one department, for example, training was an identifiable part of expenditure on the management of human resources, while in others it was an undifferentiated part of administrative budgets.
9. From April 1986, departments were to introduce the Measuring Training Activity System (developed internally to include less formal training and general support tasks among training statistics). The report found that many training branches did not use it; some had made it voluntary; only a few insisted on its completion. Reliable monitoring of the efficiency and effectiveness of training practices was, therefore, not possible.
10. In the training branches examined, trainers were drawn from the ranks of established civil servants, posted to a job as they might be to any other posting. They were not usually previously qualified trainers. There was supposed to be a uniformity of role, although there was found to be a varying emphasis in job content.

Private Sector

1. An average of 5 to 6 days per year was spent per person on training. However, the average concealed a wide variation between companies and levels of staff.
2. In a sample of leading firms, senior staff and high fliers received the most training.
3. The appraisal system, or less formalized discussion between staff and line manager, formed the basis for identifying individual needs.
4. Organizational needs were established in the course of the business planning. Performance reviews, training reviews and consultation with line managers contributed to the planning.
5. The volume and type of training received by staff varied enormously between companies. Some of them with a decentralized structure, did not keep full central records of the number of off-the-job training days received by staff. The records kept were generally of poor quality.
6. Some private sector companies appeared to attach increasing importance to assessing the impact of high priority training against overall business objectives, but their systems were still of variable quality.
7. From the information obtained, priority training areas included customer care, training in the use and application of information technology, management training, language training and general business training. Fewer than a quarter of the companies described full and systematic methods of evaluation.
8. Training budgets were normally set by negotiation on an assessment of needs and the previous years' allocations. Other factors seemed to be the perceived contribution which training made to the business objectives, and the attitudes of the chief executive. Most companies did not have complete information on their total training expenditure and the elements included in their budgets varied so widely as to make meaningful comparisons impossible.
9. Approaches to evaluating the effectiveness of training differed widely. There was an increasing trend to using business performance measures as key indicators of the impact of training. This method was judged most successful when training was designed to meet a specific business need and directed to a well-defined group of people, as in the case of customer care programmes. Other leading indicators were the selective monitoring of appraisal records and the views of the line managers. While validation and evaluation were viewed together as an important but simple operation, it did not have large resources devoted to it.

10. All companies had a central training unit which varied in size, scope and influence. Most were involved with the development of training strategies and policies and with their communication throughout the company. Some, however, were merely administrative and co-ordinating operations, while others were more active in the detailed design and delivery of training.

For the survey of private sector companies, the National Audit Office commissioned a reputable firm of accountants. It selected 14 companies, all large, with turnovers in excess of £1 billion and numbers of employees ranging from 6,000 to over 100,000. They were chosen as representative of good practice in that they recognized the importance of training to the development of their business and its employees.

Yet, despite their credentials, the companies were found to be inadequate at measuring the effectiveness or value for money of training, and the good practice they were selected for was not 'best practice'. Many readers of this book will no doubt regard their current training practice as good. Yet as my grandmother always used to quote to me:

> 'Good, better, best, never let it rest, until your good is better and your better is best!'

▶ QUESTIONS FOR THE TRAINING AUDITOR ◀

- Are you sure it's a training audit you're going to do, and not just an evaluation of training?
- Does the company have distinctive measures for economy, efficiency and effectiveness and is its definition of each the same as for the audit?
- Do you have a thorough understanding of the organization, its policies and objectives, procedures and controls, main activities and available resources? If not, where can you gain such knowledge?
- Where can training impacts be measured in cash terms, and are they measured in cash terms?
- What statistics or information are available on the current state of training in the company?

2 What is a Training Audit? What isn't it?

▷ SUMMARY ◁

- We remove the confusion, once and for all, as to what is meant by conducting a training audit. We see that it is not the process of carrying out a survey of training needs, but that it is a much broader investigation of the total systematic approach to training.
- A 12-step systematic approach to training is set out (see Figure 2.1) culminating in a 4-stage model of the Training Audit Loop (Figure 2.2). This model forms the basis for the following chapters.

What a Training Audit is not

The term 'audit' found prominence in training circles in the latter half of the 1980s. However, it has been, and continues to be, confused with activities which have been well established in training long before then.

To carry out a 'training audit' may simply mean to some that they will send a questionnaire to managers to find out what the training needs of the company are. They may even take another approach, but the end result is still the same: they have conducted a survey of training needs. Chapter 4 deals with the various ways in which needs can be identified, but a 'training audit' must go further, as Chapter 1 suggested. A training audit, then, is not a synonym for:

- Training Needs Analysis (TNA).
- Survey of Training Needs (STN).

– Company Manpower Review and Training Plan (CMRTP).
– Skills Inventories.

We tend to associate audits with the compilation of a written report. The STN and CMRTP (above) were reports which companies had to submit to their respective Industrial Training Boards (ITBs) in the UK: as many of these Boards became defunct in the latter half of the 1980s, it seemed that many companies continued the good practice of putting the document together but removed the Board's label and called it an audit – thereby identifying it for internal consumption only.

Why then can't any of these reports or surveys constitute a training audit?

Training Needs Analysis (TNA)

Traditional TNA would actually go further than the STN in identifying areas for which training solutions had to be provided. It would seek the views of managers and of individuals, and might even include observation of performance (yet usually not to the extent of competence-based performance standards, discussed in Chapter 1). Attention was given to the past and present, and this would form the basis for a reactive plan.

Survey of Training Needs (STN)

This was the term used for the initial document submitted to the ITB. It followed a framework provided by the Board and was, therefore, formalized in its approach. However, the survey simply became a summary of the results of interviews with line managers, or, at worst, questionnaires which they completed. The needs, too, as they were expressed, would be a ready prescription of the solution (which course to attend) rather than an analysis of the weakness to be addressed, or the strength to be developed.

Managers would nominate D. Fect to attend a report-writing course rather than state:

Individual	Need
D. Fect	Inability to spell and construct coherent sentences in written work.

Inevitably, real needs were not being highlighted and, therefore, the solutions provided were possibly inadequate. Again, this was very much a reactive exercise. In time, the Training Boards realized this and reformatted their requirements. The STN became the CMRTP.

Company Manpower Review and Training Plan (CMRTP)

This was really an attempt to remove the failings of the Survey of Training Needs; more work was involved but it still put the cart first. The key distinctions between the two documents were that in the CMRTP:

- Needs were considered in the light of the company's business plan, and devolved divisionally, departmentally, and individually.
- Regard was given to the future anticipated needs, so an effort was made to be proactive rather than reactive.

However, needs were still expressed as solutions, with the training plan consisting of courses with nominated delegates assigned.

The major problem with the STN and CMRTP was that, while the Industrial Training Boards reviewed each document one year in retrospect, they were only assessing how much of it was carried out and not whether it was effective.

Skills Inventories

A skills inventory is very much like a stores inventory: it itemizes what skills are currently available in a company, division or department. Left like that, though, it doesn't help training much. What is needed in addition, is what skills are actually required, and the contrast would identify potential areas for training, recruitment or redundancy. This contrast is more along the lines of a skills audit, and perhaps hints further at what an audit is. (Skills audits are addressed in more detail in Chapter 4.)

What an Audit is

In all the cases above, none of the reports commented on the ability of the training function to:

- Confirm the appropriateness of the needs.
- Provide effective solutions to meet those needs.
- Fulfil its obligation to:
  'provide the right skills or knowledge, in the right place, at the right time, to enable the company to achieve its stated business objectives.'

An *audit* can be likened to a photographic proof – a still shot in time. We examine the proof and make adjustments accordingly so that we achieve the desired result.

A *financial audit* will tell us the ability of the company to survive in the current or anticipated climate, with cash flow as the key.

A *training audit*, then, will tell us the fitness of the training function to enable the company to be where it wants to be, thereby fulfilling its obligation to the business objectives. As a result, training becomes a necessity and not the luxury that many regard it. It has to perform to a standard. Obviously, that is easier said than done.

The Prologue highlighted the typical plight of the training manager. Many books or articles have been written to say what should be done, all advocating some form of training evaluation or cost-benefit analysis. Yet most do not go as far as to tell us how to do it, or whether it can be done. While the following chapters overcome that omission in some detail (although we look at value for money rather than cost-benefit analysis), it may be helpful to have an overall picture of what is involved. To understand it fully, we must recognize what effective training involves.

What does Effective Training Involve?

The steps below outline a typical systematic approach to training:

1. Establish the business objectives of the company/organization.
2. Assess what skills are required to meet the objectives.
3. Organize those skills into functional areas (departments) each with its own set of objectives, e.g., sales, accounts, operations.
4. Recruit personnel with those skills, or the potential for them, and place them in the appropriate department.
5. Set standards of performance for each job (competences).
6. Assess the skills and knowledge of job holders against the skills and knowledge needed to fulfil the job, or to develop it further.
7. Assess the performance of the job holder against the standards of performance set.
8. Draw up a summary of the training needs of each job holder.
9. Identify or design solutions to meet those needs.
10. Implement those solutions.
11. Assess whether each need was effectively satisfied by its intended solution.
12. Redesign solutions and implement them as appropriate.

This can be summarized diagrammatically as shown in Figure 2.1.

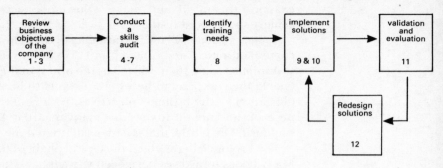

Figure 2.1 *A systematic approach to training*

What does the Training Audit Involve?

The function of the training audit is to examine the systematic approach to see:

- – How effective the approach is.
- – How well the approach works in practice
- – What changes could be made to the system and to its implementation.

So, as we can see from Figure 2.1, it requires an investigation of each stage and how each links to the other; it cannot just focus on one stage without having a likely effect elsewhere.

Looking at Figure 2.1, some worthwhile questions might be:

1. Why does the process only revert back to step 9?
2. How frequently are steps 1–8 carried out if steps 9–12 represent the training loop?
3. How certain can we be that the solution failed and not the trainee, or vice versa?
4. How much does the training policy support the business objectives of the company/organization?
5. What exactly does the validation and evaluation (step 11) take into account?

All too often the training function, for various reasons, operates from step 9 onwards – even the needs are expressed against pre-defined solutions, as we saw earlier. Assumptions are, therefore, made or imposed, that the foundation is correct. Indeed, the foundation may be correct, but unless we take a training audit we can never be sure.

It is worth noting that validation and evaluation is a step within the systematic approach which requires examination within the audit. Validation and evaluation does not, therefore, constitute a training audit in its own right, as it has often been thought to do. Figure 2.2 shows what the training audit process would, properly, look like. At any stage, findings could be fed back to effect changes in any other stage of the system.

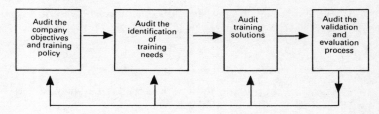

Figure 2.2 *The training audit loop*

As the redesigning of the solutions is an outcome of validation and evaluation, it has not been installed as an interim stage. Its exclusion also removes the supposition that the redesign of solutions is done without recourse to any of the earlier steps.

Also, the skills audit is just one of the ways in which needs can be identified; it will therefore come under scrutiny when auditing the identification of training needs.

Another factor requiring attention is the trainee. We should, therefore, also be auditing the trainee, but this cannot be done in isolation from the four stages already identified in the training audit loop. It will happen, instead, as a by-product of these stages; if there is a weakness in the system – whether it be the trainee or not – the training audit loop will highlight it. It looks simple enough, and so it should. However, there is much that needs comment at each stage, as the following chapters show.

▶ QUESTIONS FOR THE TRAINING AUDITOR ◀

- Is there evidence of the training having been set up on the systematic approach (as in Figure 2.1)?
- Does the training now revolve around steps 9–12 ?
- When were steps 1–8 last applied?

- Does the company still prepare a document which amounts to any of the following:
  - TNA
  - STN
  - CMRTP?
- If so, who contributes to it, how is it compiled and how is it used?

- Has any form of training audit been carried out in the past?
- Did it comply with the training audit loop shown in Figure 2.2 ?
- What was the outcome?

3 Auditing the Company Training Objectives and Policy

▷ **SUMMARY** ◁

- Shows the benefits of establishing real needs rather than delivering training for training's sake. Yet we see that even real needs are deemed to be so by relating them to the company objectives.
- Distinguishes between aims and objectives, and reviews the training policy as a reflection of the company's purpose, and as the foundation for measuring the worth of training.

The Benefits of Establishing Real Needs

The benefits of an insurance policy are never fully appreciated until a loss has been suffered, and the claim settled to your satisfaction. In the same way, to appreciate the benefits of establishing real training needs, it may be essential to experience the lack of them. The term 'benefit' implies a positive outcome, but often we may not pay as much attention to benefits as we would to pitfalls (negative outcomes). The desire for the good is nurtured by a fear of the bad.

The experience, then, of the pitfalls of failing to establish real training needs, which others have learned on our behalf, is:

1. Lack of management commitment
   This may happen because managers know that real needs are not being addressed, because the trainer hasn't consulted them. How else can he know what they are?!

2. Carefree attitude of trainees
    They think they're on a 'jolly' because their managers haven't been able to tell them the relevance of the programme to their jobs. Thus, they know that their lack of involvement is unlikely to be measurable back in the workplace.
3. Training is viewed as 'external' to the company
    Managers feel they are meeting the needs of the training department, rather than the other way round.
        As they feel it is they who are doing the supporting, they also have no qualms when they withdraw their support in times of 'economies'.
4. Lack of personal achievement
    You – the trainer – will lose your own commitment, direction, and sense of purpose. You might still be enthusiastic about the content of your programmes, but, if positive contributions to individuals and the company are not evident, you will question your own sense of fulfilment.

If these are the pitfalls, then the benefits of meeting real training needs are:

1. Commitment to training from management.
2. Involvement and commitment from trainees.
3. Training becomes indispensable and is recognized as being an integral part of the company.
4. Personal achievement.

We can also add to the above:

5. Learning is more readily identifiable and can be applied more immediately in the workplace.
6. Help is provided where it is most needed, so that training resources are not being wasted.

Where do we Start?

In Chapter 2 we highlighted the limitations of some methods of identifying training needs, and established the activity as only the eighth step in the systematic approach to training. At least it may have looked that way. In fact, what the approach does show (see Figure 2.1), is that there are seven steps to undertake before the training needs of each job holder can be summarized.

Therefore, the training audit will examine the basis on which the training needs were set, and the way in which they are expressed.

An appropriate place to start is at the beginning. So why do so many trainers start three-quarters of the way through the process at step 8? Isn't it the practice of trainers to preach the failings of making assumptions?!

A recent study conducted jointly between Price Waterhouse and Cranfield School of Management, states that: 'The analysis of business plans to identify training needs is less widely used than systems based on requests from managers and employees.'

Identity Crisis

Let us take an example of setting up a training consultancy company. Where do we begin?

The premise for wanting to start such a company may be a collection of individual talents who wish to establish a reputation for satisfying market needs. So the employees are in place and the market is made aware of the company's existence.

Business starts to trickle in and one or two consultants soon appear to be more marketable than others. This then raises the question of why? Is there a corporate identity, or is the company merely a collection of individual identities?

In which case, do the less successful consultants have a training need, or does the company have an identity crisis?

Naturally, there are many variables which come into play to answer those questions. The important thing is that the questions get asked and answered. All too readily, blame is apportioned to the individual, and that individual is targeted for the change – one way or another.

A consultancy may not be analogous with your own organization, but the likelihood is that there are departments or employees who may be operating without any focus on the corporate identity. Training is, when all is said and done, a means to achieve the company's ends, not the individual's (that would be education which is a by-product of training). As we saw in Figure 2.1, in the systematic approach,

- the functional areas of the company,
- the skills and knowledge required,
- the standards of performance for job holders,

are all devolved from the objectives of the company. After all, if you don't know where you're going, how do you know how to get there, or just as important, when you've arrived?

Company objectives should contain the why, what and how of the business.

Why?	Only when you know why the company exists (hence,
and	what it is trying to achieve) can you possibly identify
What?	what is needed to achieve it.
How?	It is not so much what we do, as how we do it. This is where the measure is found to keep the company on the right track and let it know when it has arrived.

Statement of Company Objectives

As the starting point for the training audit, it is essential that the company's objectives provide the yardstick against which we can measure the effectiveness of its activities. Very often, however, while the company will indicate where it is going, its statement of objectives will not provide the measure we're looking for. In fact, rather than a statement of objectives, it is most likely to be an expression of aims.

This would seem to challenge the majority of companies, whether large or small, who have not included such measures in their statement of company objectives. Perhaps at the time they were written, a training audit was not under consideration.

For the purpose of the training audit, though, it is essential that the company is viewed as a total package, and the audit treated as a total package. In which case there is no room for a confusion of terminology, nor for rules that apply to one part of the package but not to another. Aims should be aims, and objectives should be objectives. Furthermore, it is the company objectives we need so that we can see how effective the training function is in helping the company to achieve them.

Aims v. Objectives

To most people, these words would be considered synonymous for each other, making them completely interchangeable. As trainers, though, we would already be familiar with the specific requirement of a training objective, and we often see such objectives appearing in course brochures after the course aim has been stated. We can, therefore, define each as:

| Aim | The general direction and purpose for which something exists. |
| Objective | The specific event to be achieved while travelling in a known direction. |

Hence, objectives derive from aims. Aims are *directions*, and objectives are *destinations*. Aims are now often sub-sets of a 'mission statement'. An example of a mission statement could be:

To meet the challenge of Leadership in our industry through:

- – Quality in our team.
- – Creativity in our solutions.
- – Originality in our products.
- – Superiority in our care.

This devolves into company values, and a statement of aims. In turn these devolve into objectives. First, the values could be:

Care for our clients
and colleagues
Open to feedback
Motivation of the
team
Maintaining high
standards
Interest in the
industry
Try out new ideas
Trust in using
initiative
Empowerment to
every employee
Dedication to
professionalism

Total involvement
with the client
Optimism over pessimism
Quick to respond
Understand before
advising
Attention to detail
Loyalty to the
company
Innovation in finding
solutions
Throwing out OK
Yearning to win

The statement of company aims would refer to aspects such as profitability, growth, productivity, standards of performance, staffing and skills. Objectives would then break down each aim into expressions which define achievement. For example:

Aim   To attract, develop and retain sufficient well-trained staff with the skills to meet customer needs and expectations.

An objective   To have at least one full-time consultant who is a qualified and experienced BS 5750 trainer, registered as an approved BS 5750 lead assessor by the Department of Trade and Industry.

Consider the following, extracted from the statement of company objectives of an insurance company. Are they aims or objectives?:

1. To provide our customers with first class products and services.
2. To achieve profitable growth in order to finance the company's future, and to provide the shareholder with a competitive return.
3. To participate fully and responsibly in the affairs of the insurance industry and the local community.

There is no questioning the validity of the company's intentions, but in casting an auditor's eye over the objectives, are they *directions* or *destinations?* Are there clearly defined measures, or aren't there?

We have already shown that training is there to support the company in achieving its stated objectives. So, when will the trainers know that they have been effective in enabling the company to achieve the first objective?

Questions the training auditor must ask are:

For item 1 above
— Who dictates whether the product or service is first class? We or the customers?
— What constitutes a first class product or service? Is it defined by market share, the levels of protection offered, administrative costs, or return on investment?
— Should we be creating new products and services, or merely mimicking the best of what's available?
— How much do we want to be product-orientated, and how much service-orientated? Are they mutually exclusive or not?

For item 2 above
— Is the shareholders' competitive return dependent on the profitable growth, or vice versa?
— What is considered 'profitable' and to what extent is growth required?
— What should the shareholders' return be competitive with? What defines competitive?
— What is the company's future? Is it to maintain its position in the industry, or to obtain X market share for Y classes of business?

For item 3 above
— What constitutes full participation – is it the seniority of the employees involved, the number of employees involved, the time devoted, or the degree of impact that the company could have on the industry or community?

Where the statement of company objectives does not provide us with the measures we are seeking, we could examine to what extent the company business plans provide the answers. These should exist, and are often distributed to line management. If they don't exist, or are not commonly available to management and employees, find out why not. Also, establish how frequently financial or operating targets are set and communicated to management. Frequent changes here could require more frequent reviews of training.

The training auditor must, therefore, investigate how effectively the objectives have been delegated to the departments and job roles. Where there are gaps, duplication or misfits, corrective action must be taken by the company. The first action may be to review its business objectives.

Of course, among the departments being investigated will be training itself. Close examination must, therefore, be given to the formulation of training policy, which can only happen once the company objectives and business plan are clearly defined.

Establishing Training Policy

Many training policies, where they exist, appear to have been written to sound policy-like (often rambling and full of vague, insubstantial statements), yet they seem independent of the business objectives. If the foundation on which the house is built is not sound, then subsidence is going to appear at some stage. Then comes the choice: to make repairs or demolish it.

So how should a training policy be written? First, it must be seen to be linked to the company objectives. For example, some training policies will be a collection of statements, such as:

We will provide training:

- To all levels of staff regardless of colour, creed, age or sex.
- To enable new staff to make an immediate contribution.
- To enhance general and technical skills and increase professional standards and expertise.
- To ensure that individuals have the means to allow them to develop to their full potential.

Or it may be a single policy statement on the lines of:

The company policy is that all employees will be fully trained to the required standard in all aspects of their current jobs.

In addition to job-specific training, the company will support the development of employees so that they can fulfil their potential and contribute to the growth and profitability of the company.

The important thing about establishing policies is to plan for their evaluation at the time they are introduced. The time to consider measurement is not when looking for results, but when setting out the purpose. Consider, then, the above training policy examples against Table 3.1.

Table 3.1 *Policy statement and implementation*

Policy statement
The company's training policy is to support and encourage the development of employees so that they can attain the standards of competence required, fulfil their potential and contribute to achieving the business objectives of the company, with regard to its growth, development, profitability, and to the quality of its products and services.

Implementation
The policy is implemented through the training department whose function is:

1. To provide management with a systematic approach to training, with regard to economy, efficiency, and effectiveness.
2. To support management in the identification, implementation, administration, monitoring and evaluation of training, to achieve the stated business objectives of the company.
3. To reinforce the company's commitment to quality and its compliance to the requirements of BS 5750:Part 1:1987.
4. To ensure thorough documentation of all training activities carried out, with particular regard to the maintaining of training records.

What becomes evident is that the first group of policy statements did not reflect any consideration for the business objectives of the company, nor the significant role of line management within the training process.

Also, there was no evidence of a systematic approach and how it would be implemented. Such omissions might imply that while the mouth put the words together, the heart was not present. The role of the training auditor, we could say, is to provide the head!

The training policy statement ought to be published in the Training Policy and Procedures Manual issued to line managers. In a manufacturing concern, with an element of skilled and semi-skilled workers as well as office staff, the Manual should distinguish between the procedures which apply to job-specific training and those which relate to more general or personal skills training. The former would tend to be training of a more *ad hoc* nature, controlled and administered by the supervisors or managers, while the latter would usually be controlled through the central training department.

An example of how the Manual might be put together is shown below, with the content aiming at a 'best practice' approach. It should be noted, however, that such an approach may require the agreement of trade unions; also, it should allow flexibility for departments to devise their own procedures for job-specific training because of their diverse nature, though within a framework of control.

So, if the Training Policy and Procedures Manual includes the policy statement shown in Table 3.1, it may continue as follows:

A SPECIMEN TRAINING POLICY AND PROCEDURES MANUAL

2. *Purpose of this Manual*

The purpose of this policy and procedures manual is:

2.1   To define the systematic approach to training in respect of:
  – Job specific training.
  – General personal skills training.

2.2   To guide management in the identification of training needs, implementation, administration, and monitoring of training, to achieve the stated business objectives of the company.

2.3   To reinforce the company's commitment to quality and its compliance to the requirements of BS 5750: Part 1: 1987.

2.4   To ensure the thorough documentation of all training activities carried out within the company, with particular regard to the maintaining of training records.

3. *Procedure for Job-Specific Training*

3.1   *Definition*
Job-specific training encompasses all training activity which focuses on the technical knowledge, and skills required, for an individual to perform a particular job competently in the workplace. It does not include general personal skills training.

3.2   *Identification of Training Needs*

3.2.1 The identification of training needs is the responsibility of line managers and supervisors, who will review the performance of job holders against the standards of competence required.

3.2.2 Such reviews should take place at least annually through the Appraisal Scheme, or when departmental or job-specific objectives or working circumstances change.

3.2.3 A guide on how to identify training needs is published in the *Training Needs Analysis Workbook*, issue date ...; contact the Training Manager for further copies.

3.2.4 All training needs identified should be communicated to the job holder and agreement reached as to:
   – What the need is.
   – How and when the need can be addressed.
   The need must be expressed as a need before determining the solution, and be recorded on form, ref. no ...
      When needs have been identified and discussed with the job holder, they should be recorded in the job holder's personal file and entered into the departmental training plan.

3.3 *Implementation and Administration*

3.3.1 It is the responsibility of all line managers to compile a training plan listing:
   – The training needs against each job holder.
   – How the training needs will be met.
   – When the training should be completed.

3.3.2 Departments have their own procedures for implementing the training required and such procedures should be adhered to, with the necessary documentation maintained. However, once training has been conducted, it should be recorded against the training plan and on the job holder's training record.

3.3.3 All on-job training is to be similarly recorded, whether there has been on-job coaching, assignment work, or self-study, or any other training activity.

3.3.4 The training must only be carried out by qualified staff or those approved as instructors by line management.

3.3.5 Departments should maintain records of *all* training for job holders, noting what training was provided (cross-referencing to course content where appropriate), who provided it, and when it was conducted.

3.3.6 All training records must be readily accessible to line management or supervisors, and be kept in hard-copy format, verified by signature and date.

3.4 *Monitoring*

3.4.1 Once a job holder has received training, his/her performance must again be reviewed to ensure that the training need has been satisfactorily met. This must take place within one month of the completion of the training.

3.4.2 Should it transpire that the training has not enabled the job holder to perform to the standard of competence required, then repeat the process from 3.2.3, choosing either an alternative solution or alternative provider.

3.4.3 If, after carefully selected and appropriate training events, the job holder is still not competent to the standards required, the job holder's suitability for the job must be reassessed, or the training solutions revalidated.

4. *Procedure for General, Personal Skills*

4.1 *Definition*

General, personal skills training is that which can be transferable from one job to another and can be carried out away from the individual's workplace. It is not specific to a particular job description.

All such training will be controlled and co-ordinated by the Training Manager within a systematic approach described below.

4.2 *Identification of Training Needs*

4.2.1 The same procedure as for 3.2 should be applied. However, in addition to reviewing performance against standards of competence required, consideration must also be given to the career development of the individual and the future needs of the department.

4.2.2 The Learning Agreement shall be completed by the manager and trainee.

4.3 *Implementation and Administration*

4.3.1 Training plans should be completed as for 3.3.1.

4.3.2 As the company is sufficiently large for it to be likely that there will be a number of employees with the same training needs at any one time, many of the training solutions are already provided for through the Training Manager.

4.3.3 The Training Department publishes a *Training Brochure* for the training year from September to the end of July. This is sent to all managers so that the training needs of individuals can be set against the appropriate solution in the programme.

4.3.4 If the solutions in the programme do not seem to address the indiviudal's needs adequately, then contact the Training Department who will help you to find a suitable alternative.

4.3.5 When identifying a training solution from the *Brochure*, you must then follow the *nomination procedure* below:

(a) Complete the Course Nomination Form (ref. no. ...), ensuring that all sections are completed and all three copies of the form are legible.

(b) Retain the top copy and forward the other two sheets to your training co-ordinator, who will retain a copy and pass the remainder to the Training Department.

(c) The Training Department will co-ordinate a central training plan to allocate nominated trainees to the solutions in the *Brochure*, and will confirm course nominations, as appropriate, via the departmental training co-ordinator.

(d) All course joining instructions for participants will also be sent out via the training co-ordinators at least six weeks before the course.

4.3.6 Training records must be maintained as for 3.3.5 and 3.3.6. The Training Department will keep a central record on its own computer system.

4.4 *Monitoring*

4.4.1 Course assessment forms, ref. no ..., will be sent by the Training Department to the participants within two weeks of the course, and should be returned to the Training Department within one week.

4.4.2 The same procedure as for 3.4 should be applied.

The above specimen represents what a Training Policy and Procedures Manual could contain. However, the procedures must not only be followed, they must also be workable within the culture of the company: there may be far more involved than simply rewriting the manual.

Some things referred to in the specimen manual are commented on elsewhere in this book. If, however, changes are needed to your training policy and procedures, it is best to start with the 'best practice' approach in mind and assess the culture and practicalities against it. That way, you will have a clear indication of the challenges that lie ahead if the 'best practice' is to be attained.

► QUESTIONS FOR THE TRAINING AUDITOR ◄

- Does the company express clear business objectives, or are they merely aims?

- Is there a training policy in existence which reflects the Training Department's role as a support to management in achieving company objectives?
- Is a systematic approach to training reflected in the training policy?
- Is there evidence that the training policy is being implemented?

- Does the company have a mission statement?
- Is this devolved into values, a statement of aims, then objectives?
- Is there evidence of following the mission and adhering to the values?

- Are company business plans distributed to management, and are they regularly updated?

4 Auditing the Identification of Training Needs

> SUMMARY ◁

- Discusses six types of training need, and explores a systematic approach to identifying training needs.
- Considers advantages and disadvantages of various methods, and the importance of expressing the need correctly. Makes some distinction at this stage between the need and the solution.
- Highlights the role of line management within a 'best practice' approach to training. Points out that the identification of needs should ultimately be the responsibility of line managers rather than training personnel.
- Demonstrates, by a case study, how a skills audit could form the basis of a Training and Development Progression Plan as a step towards active training, and as a control mechanism for the provision of solutions.

Types of Training Need

Training needs can be categorized under two broad headings: reactive and proactive. These can be applied at four levels:

1. Corporate (organizational).
2. Divisional/departmental.
3. Job-centred (occupational).
4. Employee-centred (individual).

The training auditor must recognize the distinction of each and its appropriateness to the company business objectives.

Reactive and Proactive

The most commonly expressed need is the reactive one, possibly because it is easier to identify. It can often be looked on as locking the stable door after the horse has bolted. That is because it refers to reacting to things which have happened, in order to put them right.

For example, it may be that Helen Owens has been promoted to a job which requires her to make presentations in-company at management meetings. Having attempted this at two such meetings, her manager concludes that she needs to attend a presentation skills course to help her to structure her talks, to use more exciting visuals, and to instil confidence in her delivery. The manager is, therefore, reacting to correct the imbalance between what Helen is doing, and what is expected of her.

Reactive could also be considered, then, as corrective. It only caters for deficiencies in performance.

Proactive, on the other hand, is making sure the stable has a door which is lockable, before the horse is allowed in, and that someone knows how and when to apply the lock.

In Helen's case, the manager could have expressed a proactive need by saying:

> In readiness for meeting the demands of her new job, Helen should receive training in how to prepare, structure, and deliver a business presentation, so that it attains and maintains the interest of the audience, and achieves its objective.

Proactive, then, is preparatory. It requires more thought, direction, planning and, also, risk.

A true test of the worth of training in a company, is whether it has the time and foresight to look ahead, to lead the company to its mission: or, like most, it is merely occupied in catching up with yesterday's needs.

Proactive training will provide for succession planning, a desire for change, and employee development.

Corporate (Organizational)

Referring again to the first step of the systematic approach to training (Figure 2.1, page 30), we see that the organization is driven by a common mission. It therefore stands to reason that the divisions and departments will have other things in common, giving rise to shared or corporate needs.

The fulfilment of a corporate need is very much about establishing a unified identity. Like core-time in a flexitime system, it is shared by all scheme members, irrespective of how they spend the rest of their time.

A good example of a corporate need, at present, is the emergence of Total Quality Management (TQM) programmes. Unfortunately, though, while the success of such a programme depends on everyone taking part, in many companies the senior management have not considered themselves as needing the training. The training audit should, therefore, identify the falsehood of claiming a scheme as corporate, when in fact not everyone is participating.

Certain elements of an induction programme would also be 'core' to all new entrants – the company history should be the same whoever the recruit is.

Divisional or Departmental

It should be obvious that different divisions or departments performing different functions should have different needs. What may not be so obvious is that they may also share common needs.

Common needs lead to common solutions, yet all too often each division or department is left to its own devices and resources, without regard to other parts of the company. An opportunity is therefore being lost to spread the cost for training over a wider, and just as needy, audience. (However, as we shall see later, there is more to consider than just the numbers game!)

Job-centred (Occupational)

This category is often confused with that of the employee-centred, yet there are clear distinctions. This one focuses purely on the needs of the job, irrespective of the individual filling it. The individual is, therefore, viewed collectively with others doing the same job.

Hence, a firm of insurance brokers could identify time management as an obligatory programme for all its marine and aviation brokers, regardless of their age, experience and actual performance (and whether or not they had attended a similar programme with a previous employer). Some participants, then, might consider it money unnecessarily spent.

Another example, however, where money might be seen as well spent or essential for survival is where a life assurance company specifies that all its pension administrators attend a programme to update them on legislative changes as they occur.

Employee-centred (Individual)

This is the category that really matters most, yet it may not be treated with the care and attention to reflect that. Many companies would say that their employees are their most important asset. Yet they will fail none the less to recognize that employees are individuals, and individuals can differ greatly from one to the other.

For one marine and aviation insurance broker to be assumed to have the same needs as his colleague, as in the example above, without first identifying that to be the case, will ultimately end in an ineffective allocation of training resources. As we have seen earlier in the book, training is about bridging the gap between individual and organizational competences.

Implications for the audit

The audit needs to identify where the emphasis is being placed, and whether this reflects the gaps that need bridging so that the company can achieve its business objectives.

An effective training culture within an organization will have found the right balance for all four types of need. The lowest common denominator throughout, though, is the individual, so that must be where the greatest attention is given.

Then we must wait to see whether the training solutions provided succeed in satisfying these needs. If we are convinced of the validity of the needs, then it becomes easier to audit the solutions, as we see later.

How to Identify Training Needs

We can often place a need into any of the foregoing categories because of the way in which it is identified. But how does the Training Department gather up this information so that it can take the necessary action? After all, the line manager should identify the need.

The most commonly used methods employed by Training Departments are:

1. Formal interviews with the line manager.
2. Questionnaires completed by the line manager.
3. Extracting needs from the annual appraisal interview form.

For the training auditor, each of the above must beg the following questions:

    – On what basis has the line manager assessed these needs?
    – How qualified or practised is the line manager at accurately identifying needs?
    – Has the line manager already imposed a budgetary, or other constraint, so that not all real needs have been expressed?

The Managers' Responsibility

It would seem that it is the line management that is being called into question here – and so it should be. Management is the tool for implementing the policies, practices and procedures of the organization, yet it does so within the realms of specialism; sales managers, production managers, distribution managers and site managers would all be expected to be technical specialists for their own fields of expertise. They may attend specialist training programmes or management development courses as an occupational training need.

It is very much the exception, however, that any of their training has focused on their role as identifiers of training needs, and as trustees for the training and development of their staff. Some courses may give it a passing mention to remind them of this duty, but they still won't show them how it can best be done.

How often do managers receive even an introductory briefing on the company training manual? Why take the trouble, when it is easier to use the post room to distribute it, so it can serve its purpose of filling a gap on the manager's file shelf, rather than distract him from his management duties? After all, the word 'training' appears on his monthly budget returns to prompt some consideration.

Fortunately, it is not like that everywhere, though anything different is still the exception. The culture of an organization will not change overnight but will require nurturing: there are now managers coming through the ranks who have reaped the benefits themselves of training and development, and are therefore attuned to the burden of their responsibility and keen to see it through.

Having mentioned competence-based performance standards in Chapter 1, it is worth referring again to the existence of a generic set of standards for managers. The Management Charter Initiative has set units of competence for managers under the key purpose ' . . . to develop teams, individuals and self to enhance performance.' This is shown by the framework in Figure 1.1 (page 20) with their associated elements of competence.

Any company seeking good practice should require its managers to undertake that unit as a step towards accreditation and National Vocational Qualifications (NVQs). For best practice they should go further and undertake key role A2, under the generic standards for the training profession, that is ' . . . to identify the learning needs of individuals and groups.' The framework for trainers, with more background on the topic, is provided in Chapter 5.

It should mean that all training needs should reach the training department via the line managers; not the other way round.

Formal Interviews

This method is the best one at the disposal of the Training Department because it provides the platform for:

— Guiding and coaching the manager, where appropriate.
— Clarification of the manager's contributions.
— Flexibility of approach and further investigation.
— Immediate response.
— Being seen to be actively involved.
— The manager to open the discussion into areas of concern for him or her.

In many ways this may prove time-consuming and even repetitive, but we must avoid cutting corners if it is to form the basis on which everything else depends.

The purpose of the interview is to establish:

1. What the objectives for that department are?
2. Who needs training?
3. In what do they need training?
4. To what standard of performance do they need training?
5. Why do they need training?
6. When should the training be completed by?
7. Whether priority should be given to particular people or particular needs?

At this stage, any detailed discussion of solutions should be avoided. It is a fact-finding mission and not a mobile surgery. Solutions should only be considered in the light of the whole picture, which can only be seen when all line managers have had their input.

Also, while we obviously have training in mind, it may be too presumptive to refer to all needs as training needs. Training may not, in fact, be the answer. Perhaps a review of procedures or organizational change is the solution. To get the complete picture, the trainer must be aware of all needs. Yet, as regards the follow-up and accountability for satisfying those needs, the trainer should not become the dumping ground for all management's problems.

Where there is no supporting documentation at the time, these meetings are best tape-recorded. Constant note-taking can be a distraction, and key points can be misinterpreted from notes or missed altogether. Afterwards a complete and accurate document can be compiled.

Questionnaires

These should elicit the same information sought at the interview above. However, if they were to be as comprehensive as the interview, they might never get completed because it would require too much effort from the line manager. Or the manager would cut corners, thereby making the response incomplete. Alternatively, we might design a questionnaire which doesn't ask as much, and therefore doesn't help us much either!

Ideally, the Training Policy and Procedures Manual, issued to the managers, should contain a pro-forma for recording the needs of their staff within the normal course of the manager's duties. Thus, when the Training Department requires such detailed information, instead of effort being duplicated, only the form need be.

Interviews need only take place to supplement any responses which need further explanation. 'Being seen' could follow later to discuss the implications of a training plan, and the reasoning behind solutions.

Annual Appraisal Forms

Annual appraisals should review the previous year's performance against agreed objectives, then look ahead to the next year. In looking ahead, it should again agree objectives and discuss what help the appraisee may need during the year to achieve those objectives. Such help is often looked on as training, and a section of the form is labelled for these training needs to be recorded.

Unfortunately, the design of most forms, and the training of most appraisers, focuses on the solution rather than the need. If the appraiser is qualified in prescribing solutions that are the most effective in meeting the individual's need, while keeping within the needs of the organization, then there may not be a problem. In practice, this is not often the case.

The result of compiling needs from an exhaustive expedition through appraisal forms is that we end up with a list of employees against course titles (many of which could be the creation of the appraiser). As we saw in Chapter 2, not only may D. Fect be sent on a course which won't cure his problem, he may well return demoralized because the course has served to highlight his problem further.

Also, we could have a situation where the appraisee is led to believe that he will be attending a course of a certain stature, only to be sent to one he perceives to be of less standing. While the course would have been selected as being the most effective at meeting the need, it will hardly do so if he feels demoralized from the start.

For example, D. Fect is told he will be put forward to attend a supervisory skills course, yet finds himself placed on a communication skills programme instead. Although it may address his training needs, it would not fulfil the promise made to him (which would have satisfied his status needs). (To overcome such a problem the 'Learning Agreement', covered in Chapter 5, should be used.)

Management Methods

Having looked at the Training Department's approach, what methods could be used by the manager in the first place to establish training needs? They break down into the following:

1. Formal interviews with staff, usually during the annual appraisal.
2. Feedback from supervisors – following observation of performance.
3. Assessment of results against objectives.
4. Aptitude tests or psychometric testing.
5. Comparison of individual qualities against job description (usually at recruitment or induction stage).
6. Need for departmental changes as required by the business plan or external factors.
7. Company-wide directive.

Some of the above will result in reactive needs (1-4) while the other methods (5-7) demand something more proactive. Whatever method was used, the auditor requires documented evidence of how the need was assessed as well as of the need itself. This will help sort out fact from opinion as well as focus the manager's attention on proper justification of the need.

For companies seeking ISO 9001 (BS 5750 or EN 29001) status, the requirement for training is that:

– There is a systematic approach.
– Training records are maintained.

Evidence of a systematic approach is provided by the sort of documentation described. Furthermore, any document which defines the product or which may affect the quality of the product is subject to control. Ultimately the type of training given can affect the end product; so not only is it necessary to show what training was given, but also why it was given. As ISO 9001 (BS 5750 or EN 29001) is essentially a system of best practice for the production of products or services, it is complemented by the training audit which investigates the systematic approach to training more thoroughly.

More credence to the assessment of needs is likely if they are established by the supervisor's observation or a review of results against objectives. Each implies that actual performance has been assessed against recognized standards, and under normal working conditions.

Formal interviews often generate 'wants' rather than needs, while the use of tests is often construed as exam conditions leading to artificial results. Comparing an individual's curriculum vitae or characteristics against a job description looks at indicators of need other than performance measures. While it can avoid the need for corrective action later, it can also pre-judge incompetence where it may not exist.

Whether business plans and company directives are truly proactive methods depends on whether the training is carried out ahead of the implementation date for the change. If left until the change has come into effect they will then be reactive. Instead of the above choices, of course, a skills audit could be used.

Auditing the Skills Audit

Having established the aims of the company, the next logical step is to identify the skills needed to achieve the stated objectives.

In Chapter 2 we mentioned both the skills audit and skills inventory, but their references were in different contexts. A *skills audit* is where we identify the skills required to achieve known objectives. The presence of those skills contributes to best practice. A *skills inventory* is where we establish what skills exist at any time particular time. We then refer back to the skills audit to see whether we have what we need to achieve the company's purpose.

The impact of the skills audit

Essentially the skills audit is a plan which later becomes the yardstick for best practice. So it is not unlike any other audit in that respect. The difference is that the plan is documented rather than the performance against the plan (or best practice). The latter is where the inventory comes in.

If the skills audit was wrong at the outset then there are serious implications for training:

- Effort could be misdirected.
- Staff may be learning new skills which they are then unable to apply.
- The wrong skills are likely to be recruited, thereby leading to confusion and problems of morale and motivation.
- Real training needs may not be being met.
- The company may not survive for long, and training may be the first area to meet the axe.

A skills audit forms the foundation for a strategic plan. If the audit is wrong, the plan will be wrong. If the plan is wrong, the destination may be somewhere else. If we are going somewhere else, we just hope there is something en route that we recognize in time to warn us of the detour.

That is why the identification of training needs by measuring performance against company objectives, is so important. It gives us the opportunity to check the map at key points and take diversions where necessary. After all, running a business is not a mystery tour; the shorter the diversion the lower the cost, and the less time spent wondering where we are.

So, while the skills audit may have led us along the wrong road, that may not be too drastic so long as we are not reliant on it alone for formulating training plans.

Enhancing the skills audit

We have focused on the skills audit having been taken at the conception stage of the company. Obviously, this is now too late for most readers. However, it may still be appropriate to conduct such an audit, and one with added value. This time the audit could involve:

- An analysis of company functions with associated job roles.
- The setting of job roles against company employee grades.
- An analysis of core skills within grades.

The results would be:

- Job descriptions.
- Person specifications.
- A career progression plan.
- A training and development progression plan.

Such an exercise was carried out in the latter half of 1990 for a well-established insurance group. The case study at the end of this chapter describes the process and the outcome.

Timing as a Need

It would be possible for an auditor to follow through a systematic approach to see that:

- An individual's need has been correctly identified.
- The need has been correctly expressed.
- That need has been converted into a training objective.
- A solution has been designed which will achieve that objective.
- The solution has been implemented for that individual.
- The individual has since been assessed as achieving the desired standard of performance.

Yet, what if those steps within the system – from identifying the need to implementing the solution – took eight months? Is that still effective?

In Chapter 5 we shall examine what constitutes effectiveness as far as training solutions are concerned. What is reinforced, though, is that when training needs are identified an indication of the preferred time-scale for meeting the need is documented.

Case Study: Designing a Training Progression Plan

A well-established composite insurance group has been very active in meeting its training requirements, and it has expressed the commitment in its business aims to '. . . provide the conditions necessary to enable each member of staff to contribute in a measurable and rewarding way to the achievement of company objectives.' It also intends to 'ensure that individual employees are trained in general and technical skills to enable them to reach an effective level of work performance and to prepare them for progressions to posts of greater responsibility.'

It is this last statement which provides the background to the plan. Preparation for promotion is the responsibility of line management who consider continuity plans to identify development needs. However, these continuity plans are not visible to the employees, and inevitably there are some managers who are better attending to training than others. The need, therefore, is to develop a progressive, modular approach to training so that individuals can see a logical progression of training from the induction period right through to the management development higher level, and executive levels.

In essence, the group is working towards a proactive training plan, also using the occasion to redesign the training manual and resell training, and its importance, to line management.

To devise the plan, it was necessary to identify or anticipate the skills and knowledge required to function effectively at different levels of the organization. In other words, a skills audit was needed.

As the group's activities have not – despite a recent name change – altered a great deal over the last 25 years (although evolution and innovation are still taking place) job descriptions or person specifications were already in existence. Steps were taken to ensure that such descriptions and specifications were complete, and accurate. The next step was to collate the skills and knowledge requirement of each job.

Once that was complete, the job was compared to its stated grade, and a pattern emerged which highlighted between which grades the responsibilities significantly changed. This was determined by the nature of the skills and knowledge required and, from this, band-widths could be identified which represented progressive levels of training; in other words, a hierarchy of potential training needs.

For example: having set out with the preconception, if you like, of only one band-width for clerical staff, it was soon recognized that there were two levels of responsibility – processing the enquiries, and dealing with the client. This was evident from an analysis of the office skills which could be determined as 'basic' and 'advanced'. In training course terms, the two levels could not be mixed effectively without the management being accused of insulting the experience of one level, or going beyond the needs and applicability of the other.

A conflict was becoming evident between needs or solutions, which had to be acknowledged. The plan (see Table 4.1, page 60), has accompanying notes on how to use it, and a preamble from the Personnel Department, as follows:

> Clearly, within the group, there is a whole range of levels or stages of development; and within these levels people perform different roles which carry varying levels of responsibility and require different skills. In order to:
>
> – achieve high-quality performance,
> – develop the ability to progress,
>
> people need to acquire new skills and knowledge continually.
>
> We have therefore devised a Training and Development Progression Plan which anticipates the skills and knowledge required to function at the different levels of the Company. The Plan should be regarded as a progression ladder, in that each level assumes the skill requirements of the level(s) below.
>
> It should be noted that the Plan expresses the skills and knowledge required rather than simply listing the courses that

should be attended. This allows the training to fit the individual rather than the individual to fit the course, and gives us greater flexibility over the design and provision of training solutions.

A few points can be drawn from this:

1. The plan is a working guide against which line management assesses needs. (The training manual has a section devoted to helping the manager to identify needs and effect the training.)
2. Adhered to, it is equivalent to an on-going skills audit (which will need changing as the group's activities change).
3. The plan, while identifying progression, can be used reactively as well as proactively.
4. It makes the designing of in-house courses easier.

That last point is certainly worth noting, because the plan does help with the solutions.

A Group the size of London and Edinburgh Insurance can reasonably expect quite a number of staff to have similar skills needs at the same time – sufficient, in fact, to run a programme of training in-house.

By looking at the grouping of skills in their band-width, it is possible to design courses combining associated skills from that grouping, so that more effective use can be made of time and resources, and possible duplication of content can be avoided. For example, rather than having staff attend a course on planning and organizing and then another on delegating, the two could be combined. The distinction between planning the work and working the plan could be linked to a live project, and further lessons learned.

For the above reasons, a number of courses have been designed in-house which are likely to meet real needs at particular levels of the company. These are listed in the column headed 'Off-Job Training', in Table 4.1.

The preamble also points out that:

Certain courses are highlighted and these are the core courses which we would expect will be generally applicable to the majority of staff at that level.

However, some of these core courses are specifically aimed at developing man-management or supervisory skills and are therefore obviously applicable to those who have, or are likely to have, management/supervisory responsibilities.

In conclusion then, let us say: if the Matrix is to be properly used, it must be seen as a general guide, and not something cast in tablets of stone. The individual's needs, in certain cases, will differ from the needs of his/her peer group. This is where you, the Manager, play a key role in the development of your staff:

OPEN/EXTERNAL COURSES

It can happen that the objectives of the pre-designed Training Courses do not suit the training needs of the individual:

- Perhaps he/she only needs training in one of several areas offered by a course, in which case spending 3 days on the complete course would be largely a waste of time.
- Perhaps he/she needs training in a skill area not offered by any of the courses, e.g. Rapid Reading.

When that is the case, contact Personnel who will try to arrange for the individual to attend an external course more tailored to meet his/her needs.

In addition, we see that it is easier to review the content of an external provider's set programme against current needs than against other less certain or less meaningful criteria. The exercise certainly highlighted one or two instances where the programme being delivered was probably not what was needed. This was not a criticism of the provider, but it was found that some of the skills taught in one management level programme were appropriate then, but other skills were not required yet or had already been dealt with elsewhere. The course may still prove enjoyable and constructive, but much of the learning cannot be applied and may therefore be dissipated altogether.

The pitch of training, and levels of participants, are much easier to determine: the course may have the same label but the subject could be approached entirely differently according to the level. For example, a time management course may focus at one level on how to set priorities and delegate. At another level, the priorities may already be determined for you, and at another there may be no-one to delegate to.

Corporate issues and qualifications

The commentary so far has concentrated on the skills aspect of the plan, labelled as career skills and support skills. Essential skills are those required to function at the level shown: skills required by only some staff are identifiable with particular roles within those grades. Corporate issues refer to more knowledge-based requirements, or skills which are not related specifically to the job but to 'extra-curricular' activity. Qualifications are those desirable within each band-width, and which may, depending on the technical nature of the job, be a prerequisite for the job.

59

The plan below represents the minimum skills which the Group would expect of its employees at the various levels. It should be regarded as a progression ladder, in that each level assumes the skill requirement of the level(s) below.

LEVEL	PRINCIPAL RESPONSIBILITIES	CAREER SKILLS	
		ESSENTIAL SKILLS	SKILLS REQUIRED ONLY BY SOME STAFF MEMBERS
EXECUTIVE	Planning/Directing Corporate Policy and Corporate Strategy	Stragetic Planning Competitive Analysis Identifying the Need for Change	
GRADES 16-18	Managing the Business	Major Project Management Managing Change Planning and Implementation Budgeting and Finance Managing Pressure	
GRADES 13-15	Achieving Results through/with others	Negotiating Skills Staff Development Problem Solving Managing Meetings Personal Effectiveness Team Building Leadership Dealing with Staff Difficulties Delegation Planning & Organizing Decision Making Self Development Presentation Skills	Influencing/Selling Skills Selection Interviewing Presentation Skills Counselling
TECHNICAL ADMINIS-TRATIVE AND SUPERVISORY	Taking Responsibility for the task team and self	Appraisal Technical Skills Feedback Skills Time Management Handling Criticism Motivation Coaching Monitoring	Report Writing Skills Technical Skills
SENIOR CLERICAL	Advanced Processing Dealing with Clients	Assertiveness Handling Complaints Effective Letter Writing	
CLERICAL	Processing Dealing with Enquiries	Telephone Techniques Active Listening Office Practices Being an Effective Team Member	

Table 4.1 *Training and development progression plan*

Some progressive training solutions
The right-hand column represents some solutions currently available to provide the training identified on the Progression Plan. Further details for each appear in the Off-Job Training section of this manual.

SUPPORT SKILLS	CORPORATE ISSUES	PROFESSIONAL QUALIFICATIONS (EXAMPLES)	OFF-JOB/TRAINING	
	Overview of the industry		ITT Courses: General Management Business Strategy Advanced Management Programme	Industry Seminars Conferences
	Overview of the Group	FIA FFA FCA	EFFECTIVE SENIOR MANAGEMENT LEADERSHIP TRUST Suitable open/external courses	
Capex Parex Profile	'Tutor' Skills Individually-Tailored Induction	Studying for/ holding FCII ACCA or equivalent	Personal Development Effective Presentation Skills Time Manager Suitable open/external courses FIRST-LINE MANAGEMENT	Capex Parex Training
from [Lotus Multimate Softplan Story-board DOS	Company Induction	Studying for/ holding ACII AAT	Report Writing Skills Appraisal Skills Female Focus INTRODUCTION TO SUPERVISION External/Internal Administration/Technical Training	Introduction to Reinsurance
Keyboard Skills Use of Company Telephone System Use of Email	Departmental Induction Introduction to the concepts of Insurance	Btec CP	ADVANCED COMMUNICATION SKILLS Letter Writing Skills	Introduction to Insurance
			OFFICE COMMUNICATION SKILLS	Office Systems Training

Table 4.1 *Continued*

In summary, the plan provides a visible framework against which training can be provided to meet the core skills of the group. It is used as a supplement to the individually-tailored plans which departments operate, and which cater more fully for the technical requirements of the job.

► **QUESTIONS FOR THE TRAINING AUDITOR** ◄

- Which of the following methods are employed by managers to identify training needs:

    - Annual appraisals?
    - Observation of performance (via supervisor)?
    - Assessment of results against objectives?
    - Aptitude tests or psychometric testing?
    - Comparisons of individuals to job description?

- Are the managers all trained in the techniques for identifying training needs?
- Is there a positive management attitude to training?
- Is the method of identification consistent throughout the company or are there wide variations?

- Does the company operate a scheme of competence-based performance standards?
- If so, what are the levels of competence and for whom are they set?
- How is assessment carried out?
- Is it linked to the appraisal scheme?
- Does a comprehensive Training Policy and Procedures Manual clearly show managers the procedures to follow for:

    - Identifying training needs?
    - Putting training into effect?
    - Validation?
    - Monitoring and evaluation?

- Have managers completed unit of competence I5 of the Management Charter Initiative, or key role A2 from the occupational standards for the training profession?
- What documentation is available and implemented within the systems approach to training?
- Is the company approved for ISO 9001 (BS 5750 or EN 29001)?

- Are there any succession plans or training and development progression plans in effect?
- Are these done for every department and/or are they co-ordinated centrally?

- Is there a training plan compiled for each department, and is it for one year or up to five?
- Are the plans complete and consistent throughout the company?
- Are all employees considered within the plans?

---

5 Auditing the Training Solution

 ▷ SUMMARY ◁

- Solutions are usually the criteria by which training effectiveness is measured. However, it will now become clear that there is more to look at than the solutions alone.
- Solutions should not be viewed in isolation but within the scheme of things. We should always question, not just the needs being satisfied, but the methodology being employed.
- A model – the Effectiveness Triangle – has been created to show the relationship and degree of influence of economy, efficiency and frequency in determining the effectiveness of solutions.
- Explores the pros and cons of different training methods, and looks at the role of the trainee within the solution and why the concept of a Learning Agreement should be promoted.
- Provides a brief sample of the occupational performance standards devised for the training profession by the Training and Development Lead Body in the UK, as a contribution to 'best practice'.
- Concludes with a case study which shows the problem which can arise when needs are seen only in the light of predetermined solutions. It also shows how a receptive and open-minded approach can reap benefits.

A Question of Motivation

One of the most common failings of trainers can be our belief that we are employed only to run courses, and that we were taken on because of our particular specialisms. Two things, therefore, which can immediately limit our effectiveness, are self-inflicted. Believing that we exist only to run courses can distract our attention from other perhaps more worthwhile solutions, and, in acknowledging our own specialisms, we can be deluding ourselves into thinking that we must incorporate that specialism in the courses we offer.

We all have our pet subjects and preferred way of doing things, but are we not occasionally guilty of self-indulgence at the expense of the trainee? Our own limitations, where we are seen as in-house providers, restrict the flexibility and reliability of training. The previous chapter left us in no doubt that a solution is not a solution until it meets the needs of the trainees, which in turn satisfies the attainment of company objectives. It is only right, therefore, that in auditing the training solution, the motivation that guided the trainer to that solution should be questioned.

An inadequate training solution may also be the result of:

- Incorrectly defined needs of the company.
- Incorrectly defined needs of the target audience.
- Poor training design.
- Faulty implementation/delivery.
- The wrong 'mix' of trainees.

However, one question which should obviously be asked but usually isn't, needs attention before we investigate the above causes: 'How do we know whether the solution succeeded or failed?' Success or failure is not solely a matter of whether it meets or doesn't meet the needs. It is more a matter of measurement and evidence of that measurement.

Let us take the situation referred to in Chapter 2, where D. Fect has been earmarked for training which will help him overcome his 'inability to spell and construct coherent sentences in written work'. We have already acknowledged that his inclusion on a report-writing programme may not have been appropriate – what we must ascertain is the extent of the gap between his inability and what the company would accept, in terms of correct spelling and construction of coherent sentences in written work.

In other words, we sample the 'before' against the desired model. At the end of the training we sample the 'after' against the desired model to see that they match, (within defined and accepted tolerance levels perhaps). We then have something against which we measure performance, and hard evidence of that new performance.

Contrast this with the situation where a solution was already in existence to meet that very same need for somebody else. On that occasion it proved very effective in enabling the trainee to achieve the new standard of performance sought. So the solution could be deemed a success because it met the particular need.

D. Fect undergoes the same training, but does not achieve the desired standard of performance. Is the very same solution still a success? In short, a solution can only be defined as such after each event, and not before. What the designer must do, however, is significantly increase the chances that it will succeed.

Education or Training?

When training people to make successful business presentations, it is helpful to them to draw on the distinctions between a presentation and a lecture. Such distinctions are also relevant in focusing our attention on the requirements for a training solution, as Table 5.1 shows.

Lecture	*versus*	*Presentation*
One-way		Two-way
Tell		Sell
Subject-orientated		Audience-orientated
The audience's need to attend is greater than the lecturer's need to lecture.		The need to present is often greater than the audience's perceived need to attend
Can command attention		Has to deserve attention
The lecturer can give homework out		Has to do the work to make it easier for the audience to follow
The lecturer asks: 'How long does the subject need?'		The presenter asks: 'How long can the audience spare?' 'How long can I expect to keep their attention?'

Table 5.1 *Lecture versus presentation*

An effective training solution should be akin to a presentation, as above, and not to a lecture, because it addresses the needs of the audience rather than just those of the subject itself. In that case, you may ask, why are lectures always identifiable with education establishments?

My own view is that the differences between the two methods also distinguish education from training. Education is concerned with imparting knowledge and assessing, through examinations, a person's ability to learn; training, on the other hand, focuses more on a person's ability to apply the learning. Another contrast between education and training is that in the former, responsibility for learning rests with the student, while in the latter the trainer is considered more accountable.

That is not to say that there aren't any conscientious teachers, or that all trainers would blame themselves and not the trainee. In defence of the educationalists, it is only fair to add that most college or university lectures would be followed by a tutorial; this is where the two-way process can operate, but it is mostly up to the student to seek clarification.

Confusion is created, however, because there may be lecturers whose style makes them presenters, and in the business environment there are numerous events called presentations, which are more akin to lectures. None the less, the essence of designing a training solution is that it:

- meets the needs of the audience rather than solely the subject.
- involves the audience.
- convinces the audience of why things are a particular way.
- doesn't swamp the audience with too much information too quickly.
- incorporates tests of learning at key stages, against which desired changes of performance can be measured.
- creates the environment where the audience feels free to exchange information, ideas, and questions.

Involving the audience in a presentation may only go so far as to allow them to ask, or answer, any questions. In training, we should involve our audience physically, as well as mentally. We should all be aware that we learn more by doing – but listening to the trainer and asking him or her questions is not what the advice has in mind. Such advice is supplied by:

I hear	and	I forget
I see	and	I remember
I do	and	I understand

If learning is the ability to recall from memory, why do many training solutions appeal only to the ears? Once more, then, we look to objectives to guide us to the most appropriate solution.

Expressing a Training Objective

A training objective is merely a statement which identifies what the trainee will have achieved, having undergone a training event. In other words, it is a focus on the measurable outcome of the training, rather than just a list of objectives that the training addresses.

The training objective should not derive from the content of the solution: it should be the other way round. It is the training need which gives rise to the training objective, and so a properly expressed need should make expression of the corresponding objective that much easier to do. For example:

The need: To operate the capstan-lathe.
The objective: By the end of the training the trainee will be able to:

– operate the capstan-lathe effectively.

This example does not give us the measurable outcome, even with 'effectively' tagged on the end. We would still require a measure of what effective is.

If, however, the need had been more correctly identified as:

– To operate the capstan-lathe safely and with no worse that a 3 per cent error rate

it could give rise to more than one objective which the trainer could express and accomplish within a single training session.

So, by the end of the training, the trainee will be able to:

– Recall and apply the guidelines of the Health and Safety at Work Act (HASWA) 1974, as related to capstan-lathes.
– Operate the capstan-lathe so that the error rate is no worse than 3 per cent.

Earlier in the book we commented on the distinction between an aim and an objective. Training objectives are usually prefaced with the phrase:

'By the end of the training, the trainee will be able to . . . '

It helps the mind to focus on the outcomes and allows each particular measure to be listed.

An aim, on the other hand, would be more of an overall activity statement without the measure, such as:

– This training will enable trainees to operate the capstan-lathe more effectively.

Unfortunately, many programme outlines refer to objectives which are really aims. This may usually reflect that it is a case of the supply waiting to attract some demand. (See Chapter 3 for the distinction between aims and objectives.)

What should be borne in mind with training solutions is that there are at least two parties involved – the designer and the trainee. As it is the designer who writes the training objectives, there is always the chance that they will get carried away with looking at the solution from their own point of view, looking at his or her own input rather than at the direct outcomes.

This can be likened again to a business presentation. For the presenter to state at the opening of the presentation that the objective is: 'To tell you about the activities of the computer department and about the hardware used in the company,' may justifiably leave the audience asking themselves: 'Why? What's in it for me? Why should I listen?'

He or she has told the audience why he or she is there, but not why *they* are there. Yet they should be there for a purpose, or not at all. If they know what is expected of them by the end of the presentation, they can listen with purpose and question with genuine interest and concern.

To facilitate this, the presenter should give the audience its own objective. He or she could link it to the presenter's objective with three words: '... so that you ... ' The two combined give us the objective of the presentation – which is, therefore, not the same as the presenter's objective.

For the same situation, then, the objective of the presentation would be complete if it were:

> To tell us about the activities of the computer department and about the hardware used in the company ... *so that you* ... can identify areas where we can help you, and can accept the reasons why we believe the systems we use will satisfy the needs of the company for the next fifteen years.

Immediately, the audience can set aside mental pigeon holes in which to gather information relevant to what is expected from them. Namely:

Pigeon hole 1 – Activities which could be of help.
Pigeon hole 2 – How the help could be organized.
Pigeon hole 3 – The company's needs over the next 15 years.
Pigeon hole 4 – The computer system's suitability to those needs.

Where such information is not supplied, the audience can ask questions to elicit what they need – even if they finally conclude that the computer department cannot help them.

Training solutions should apply the same principle. They should identify the trainer's intentions or input, as well as the specific outcomes expected of the trainees.

One way of ensuring that the trainees know exactly what is expected of them, is to use a practice such as the Learning Agreement.

The Learning Agreement

In the ideal world, this would already be in use as common sense and good practice. While in some companies management has applied the principle, it is still an aspect that is not supported by any structured or formal documentation.

It has always astonished me that although we document the identification of needs, and keep training records and copies of training solutions, the only thing that links them together is the trainee, who has no chance to record his or her involvement until the course assessment form is handed out. It is no wonder that trainees turn up on courses unsure of why they are there.

Many is the time people have turned up for a presentation skills workshop who say they don't make presentations, or on report-writing courses, when they don't write reports. It would not have been so bad if there had been at least the prospect that they were being prepared for a change of role. Sadly, no one had told them if that was the case.

Much success of training can be attributed to the commitment of the trainee. It often seems, though, that the trainee's own line manager ought to be the one committed! Where such instances as that above occur, it often betrays that line management measures training by numbers. Management feels it has done its training more effectively by putting 20 people through a programme, rather than 12. This is particularly evident where external consultants are providing the training.

Value for money is determined by minimizing the cost per head of the training, against the consultancy fee. This, as we know now, is misguided, for value for money, as identified in the Introduction, not only looks at economy but at efficiency and effectiveness as well.

It takes only one discontented and uncommitted group member to threaten the success and effectiveness of a course. We would expect professional trainers to be able to limit this disruptive influence, and even generate some commitment: but they can't be in all places at once, and refreshment breaks and syndicate work is when much of the negative element can be injected.

PERSONAL DEVELOPMENT PLAN → → → *DISCUSSION AND REVIEW* → →

Course Title:	
Date:	
Time:	
Venue:	

THE LEARNING AGREEMENT

Getting the most from the Course

depends on _____ (Participant)

and _____ (Manager)

Extracts from the Learning Agreement have been reproduced with the permission of Godfrey Durham Training Consultants Ltd.

Figure 5.1 *The Learning Agreement*

Why a Learning Agreement?

■   The Eight Step Learning Agreement is designed to help you to prepare for and review the course:

> · what you expect
>
> · what you have learned
>
> · what you have used

■   It's also an opportunity to discuss your views with your manager

The Course Aims/Objectives

Figure 5.1 *continued*

BEFORE THE COURSE

WHAT DO YOU WANT FROM THE COURSE?

This booklet offers you the opportunity to ensure that both you and your manager obtain the maximum benefit from the training course you are planning to attend

Just before the course arrange to meet your manager to share your expectations

1.   Consider the course aims and objectives on p.71. How do you expect to benefit *personally* from attending this course?

2.   How does your *manager* expect you to benefit from attending this course? What training need(s) is the course aiming to resolve for you?

Figure 5.1 *continued*

PUTTING INTO PRACTICE

WHAT ARE YOU GOING TO DO AS A RESULT OF THE COURSE?

*Consider your previous
expectations*

*Consider any new expectations
you have identified*

3.   What have you learned from the course that you will put into
practice?

When?

4.   What support do you think you will need in the future to help you put
what you have learned into practice?

Figure 5.1 *continued*

ONE MONTH AFTER THE COURSE

WHAT HAVE YOU ACHIEVED AT WORK AS A RESULT OF THE COURSE?

Approximately one month after the course, arrange to meet your manager

Review the course benefits

5.   What did you learn on the course which you have been able to put into practice? How?

6.   What have you been unable to use from the course? Why?

7.   Have your manager's expectations of the training you received been fulfilled?

8.   What further help can your manager or the company offer you?

Figure 5.1 *continued*

The Learning Agreement (Figure 5.1) is the documented process of bringing together the prospective trainee and his supervisor or line manager, to discuss the need for the training and the desired outcome.

The following benefits can be derived from the Learning Agreement:

1. The manager is prompted to justify the training needs identified.
2. The trainee is prepared for the training, because he recognizes the need and knows what is expected of him.
3. The trainee can be more convinced of the appropriateness of the solution and, therefore, more committed to it.

   Also, there is less chance of the manager putting up barriers afterwards to prevent the trainee from applying what he or she has learned.
4. It usually provides a more frequent opportunity to discuss the individual's performance than the annual appraisal system does.
5. It builds in a monitoring of the change in performance following training:
   - It establishes what has been learned.
   - It establishes what has been implemented.
6. Further training can be highlighted and discussed, where appropriate.

This Agreement should be as much a part of the solution as the training itself. Trainers should promote and recommend its use at every opportunity.

Figure 5.1 only reflects a base format for the Learning Agreement, as it can be tailored to specific training events, and not just courses. It will prove effective, though, only when managers and supervisors are trained in how to apply it and how to convince the trainees, too, of its purpose.

Too many well-intentioned ideas die in transit through the post room, instead of receiving a stimulating injection at a gathering of management blood donors. If the Training Department is not prepared to devote time and energy to the proper launch of new procedures, it is hardly surprising when managers perceive such changes as having little or no value, and that Training has produced more paperwork chores to justify its existence. That is, if they even know the new procedure is available.

Added value is achievable from the Learning Agreement when the training provider is also party to it. The trainer could make time available in the programme for referring to the Agreement, to focus the mind of the trainee and the trainer, and to ensure that trainees' objectives are being met. Prevention is, after all, better than cure.

A Model Solution

Each method of training has its own advantages and disadvantages, so obviously the method used to satisfy particular training needs is a factor in the success of training. What the auditor should be looking for is the criteria against which selection of the solution was made.

The most important factor should be that it addresses the learning objectives for a known category of trainees. The needs have therefore been identified and translated into measurable standards of performance, as we saw earlier in the Chapter.

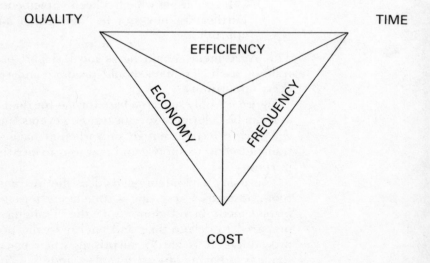

Figure 5.3 *The effectiveness triangle*

What other criteria may there be, then? Perhaps the cost, then the size of the trainee group, and how long the training would take. Perhaps it had to make use of existing resources or match somebody's pre-ordained format. Consider the model shown in Figure 5.2 and the relationship between the criteria. The factors at play are seen as quality, cost, and time. If the triangle can be applied to a training solution, we would see the influence of each by the size, and therefore shape, of the three individual triangles.

Ideally, a balance of all factors would leave us with three identically sized and shaped triangles. The point Y would have to be in the very centre of the equilateral triangle. Such a relationship would represent complete effectiveness of the solution, in design terms at least.

However, if too much emphasis were given to economic constraints, the economy triangle would increase in size and, therefore, reduce the solution's efficiency and frequency. Without the Y at the very centre of the equilateral triangle, effectiveness of the solution is not achieved.

What could be meant by the terms economy, efficiency and frequency within the context of the solution, and what factors determine their contribution?

Economy

We saw, in Chapter 1, that economy is concerned with minimizing the cost of resources acquired or used, having regard to quality.

If we take the example of a proposed solution to address customer-care needs, the trainer, having examined the needs and standards of performance required, might decide that the best solution is a two-day course with no more than ten trainees per course. This is so that customer-service skills can be practised by each participant and not just talked about in a group.

What cost considerations are there? Obvious ones would be the direct costs such as:

- Paying an external consultant, if used, or the trainer's salary at a daily rate.
- Hiring films, materials or equipment.
- Paying trainer's and trainees' expenses.
- Producing handouts or materials.

Possibly not so obvious are the indirect costs, which are likely to be:

- Loss of productive time while participants are away from their jobs.
- Delayed or lost business while participants are not contactable by customers.

So, if it became a case of putting 16 trainees on the course to spread the other costs more, while the economy factor increases, there are likely to be detrimental spin-offs to efficiency and frequency.

Efficiency may reduce because the trainer can no longer devote as much time and attention to each individual, and the putting into practice of theory may be curtailed for logistical reasons.

Frequency will reduce because it will not be necessary to run as many courses. Instead of 16 courses with 10 people on each, there will be only 10 courses with 16 on each.

Hence, as the three internal triangles are no longer of equal size, the Y will not be in the centre; efficiency will therefore be sacrificed for economy, resulting in a less than completely effective solution. This would therefore be considered a false economy. A true economy would be to reduce the overhead or per capita cost by:

– Finding an equally competent trainer at less cost.
– Providing the same films, materials or equipment at less cost.
– Using someone else's budget to cover expenses.
– Producing the handouts to the same standard, but at less cost.

Efficiency

Our definition of efficiency contrasted the measure of output with a given measure of input, so that output was maximized. In the customer care example, the trainer represents one given item of input. Others would be:

– Content covered.
– Films or materials used.
– Equipment used.
– Time taken.
– The participants themselves

Output would be the ability of the participants to meet the standards of performance required from the training.

Maximum efficiency would be when the required output is attained with the minimum of input for any specific training solution (each course can be taken independently).

Let us consider, then, the impact on efficiency of changes to some of these inputs. One of the training objectives of the course is to enable the participants to apply certain techniques so that they can handle incoming complaints on the telephone, without antagonizing customers further but gaining their confidence instead.

The trainer had recommended a two-day programme with 10 trainees. His plan was to discuss with them the correct approach to such calls, then provide them with the opportunity to practise that approach. They were to spend an afternoon dealing with typical calls, using telephone role-play equipment, which caters for five pairs at a time. Each trainee would get three opportunities to apply and absorb what he or she had learned.

If management were to dictate that 16 trainees attend each course, what would be the likely impact on efficiency? Can the same output still be achieved with the increased input? Will the increased input create a discernible increase in output?

There is a distinct possibility that any of the following could occur:

1. The training objective for handling complaints on the telephone could still be addressed, but trainees will get only one chance to put the theory into practice during the course.
2. The timetable is adjusted so that each trainee still has three opportunities to put the theory into practice.
3. The training objective is dropped from the course.
4. The training objective is covered through the use of a film and discussion only.

Each of the above decreases the efficiency of the course, suggesting that the course is not being done the right way. Let us see why this is so.

If trainees get only one chance to put the theory into practice, there is a greatly reduced chance that they will actually possess the skills or techniques to achieve the desired outcome. The defence that practice will continue when dealing with live calls in the workplace may prove costly. The whole point of the training simulations is that mistakes can be made without suffering the consequences that the real event could bring. The culprit, too, may still learn from the mistake, without loss of face, or possible loss of job prospects.

The impact of changing the timetable is that something else in the course has had to change to make the time available for three practices each. Hence, there has been a compensating reduction in input, so that output may be less than maximum. It may be that another training objective, which could have been achieved previously, has been removed or had its chances of achievement weakened by reducing practice time.

Certainly output will be less than maximum if the objective is dropped altogether, and the company may still be losing potential custom or tarnishing its image. While input has decreased for that objective, it may be replaced by an increase in input for another objective.

Knowledge can be gained through discussion and film, but skills must be practised. So the use of these would lead to the same problems that a lack of practice time presented. The 'deep end' may prompt some learners to swim sooner than they would like, but could companies bear the liability damages from the occasional drowning?!

If, on the other hand, the course had been conceived with 16 trainees but was later enhanced to 10, this would have had the effect of improving efficiency. The same output could be achieved with less input. The original design may already have had more than its fair share of economy.

But while the logic leads us to conclude that it would be more efficient to have one trainee attend the course at a time, spare a thought for what this would do to economy in the effectiveness triangle (Figure 5.2). The Y would be far from central, indicating that operational goals and other intended effects were not being achieved.

Frequency

The relationship between cost and time would be termed productivity when looking at performance measures. A more accurate term in the context of training solutions would be 'frequency'. Both economy and efficiency would have an impact on it as they, too, are affected by cost and time. For example: if a course cost £1,200 to put on, then four courses could be run in a given year for less than £5,000.

Let us say, though, that economies are needed, or imposed, and there is only £3,000 to spend. Obviously, four of those courses cannot be run within that budget, nor can three. So the frequency of courses in one year is reduced. Frequency has conceded territory to economy.

Alternatively, the budgetary constraint may lead to a redesign of the course, affecting the relationship between input and output, as discussed earlier. Thus, to maintain the original share of frequency, the cost of each course must come down to £750, so that four could be run within the £3,000 budget. Frequency is then able to regain some of the territory it lost to economy, while efficiency, too, regains some stature to enhance overall effectiveness.

Value for Money

We have related the effectiveness triangle (Figure 5.2) to a course-style solution. The principle, however, applies just as readily to the design of distance-learning material, where frequency is the number of learning packs in use at a given time.

It is virtually impossible to qualify statistically the degree of impact that any change in one segment has on the other two. Its value, though, is in applying 'what ifs' to recognize the relationship of all three components – economy, efficiency, and frequency – to the primary target for achievement, namely effectiveness.

That is how we can take steps to increase significantly the chances that a solution would succeed, not just as a training experience, but as something that represents value for money.

Other influences

The training auditor will benefit from having some knowledge of training techniques, but he or she should not be too worried where this knowledge is lacking. For there should be in existence, and readily available, documentation with information on:

- The objectives a solution was designed to meet.
- The number of trainees it is intended for at any one time.
- The type of trainee it is aimed at.
- The duration of the learning.
- The specific content covered (though not to the extent of a script).
- The methodology employed to achieve the objectives.
- The relevant knowledge, skills and experience of the trainer.

As we saw in the previous Chapter, there should also be documentation to highlight the needs for the solution in the first place. (In case of need, however, see pages 53-4.)

Methodology

The auditor should explore the methodology of the solution to see whether it could be improved. He or she needs to establish from the documentation if, and why, exercises, practicals, films, discussion, role-plays, handouts and materials were used.

If the objective of a solution were to provide the trainee with certain skills, why were only film and discussion featured? Or, what was the value of incorporating fun activities which seem to bear no relevance to the objectives?

More often than not, however, such documentation as described above is not available. The auditor should therefore recommend that it becomes a requirement for all future solutions, and for those already in existence. This would be advantageous for companies seeking ISO 9001 (BS 5750 or EN 29001) approval.

Where documentation is not available, Table 5.2 provides a guide for the auditor to the pros and cons of more commonly used training methods:

Table 5.2 *The pros and cons of commonly used training methods*

Method
Lecture
PROS

A lot of material can be covered fairly quickly.

Almost no limit to the numbers in the audience.

The lecturer is not distracted by trainee interaction.

CONS

Lack of active participation for the trainee.

I hear and I forget!

The trainee attention span is easily surpassed.

No immediate feedback for the lecturer.

Discussion
PROS

Attention can be gained in short bursts.

Less to remember in one go.

Trainees can participate and get answers to questions.

Can remove the classroom syndrome

CONS

Must be well-controlled to avoid losing its purpose.

Trainees must have basic relevant knowledge if they are to contribute/ask questions.

Can be time-consuming.

Film
PROS

Can create interest and variety.

Provides 'fly on the wall' learning.

Trainees can see the theory in practice.

Action can be speeded up, slowed down, or frozen.

CONS

Can be expensive to produce, buy or hire.

Can soon appear dated.

May not be adaptable to different trainee groups.

Trainees may be distracted by the actors/actresses, locations, or construction of the film.

Needs careful introduction.

Exercises:
– Case study
PROS

Involves trainees mentally.

Trainees can use their knowledge and experience.

Can be tailored to elicit specific learning points.

CONS

Needs careful design and application.

May not be 'real' enough.

Answers may not be 'black and white' so conclusions may be hard to draw.

— In-tray

PROS

Resembles work activities.

Can be designed to draw out a variety of learning points.

Offers a more direct measure of a trainee's competence.

Can be 'real' activities with the names changed.

CONS

Can be time-consuming to produce.

Can get bogged down in internal politics.

May be viewed as nothing new, and interest lost.

— Business Games

PROS

Very participative.

Builds competitive edge.

Participants can identify their own strengths and weaknesses during the game.

Learning can be hastened.

Feedback can be more immediate.

Can be real without real consequences.

CONS

Competition may be more dominant than learning.

May lose appeal for non-mathematicians.

Failure can lead to loss of face.

Time-consuming to create.

May be excused as artificial — 'yes, but in the real event ...'

Coaching

PROS

A one-to-one relationship focuses all attention on the trainee.

Approach can be flexible.

Immediate feedback of learning.

No threat for trainee of losing face in front of colleagues.

CONS

The coach must have time and show patience.

Personalities play a bigger role and clashes can result.

Takes longer to meet the needs of larger groups.

Role-plays

PROS

Can get close to reality.

Draws out knowledge, skills-attitudes, behaviours, emotions.

Generates involvement.

Can learn by doing and observing.

Enhances empathy for different roles.

Can have element of fun.

CONS

Can be construed as artificial.

Tendency for participants to seek Oscar nominations and obscure the learning.

All trainees must be actively involved either as role-players or observers.

Distance Learning Packages

PROS	CONS
Trainee can learn in own time and place.	Trainee may have questions which the package doesn't answer.
Trainee can dictate pace of learning.	Requires self-discipline of the trainee.
Standardizes learning.	No immediate feedback to the trainer/manager.
Everyone gets the same message.	
No need to wait for a quota of trainees before training begins.	Can lack flexibility for different individuals.

There are other training methods, of course, and other books which explore them in more detail. A summary, though, of key points for the auditor to note is:

- The average attention span is no more than twenty minutes.
- One-way communication may be quicker but proves less effective.
- Activity and discussion are slower but they reinforce learning.
- Films, case studies and syndicate exercises need careful introduction and review.
- A lack of variety and enjoyment is not conducive to learning.

For example, there may be nothing more sleep-inducing for trainees to attend than a poorly designed company induction programme. Perhaps that is how it got the name.

The majority of them conjure up visions of 12 or more employees undergoing an endurance course. They are talked at over two days typically, in sequences of 45-minute lectures. What could be worse? Well, a sequence of 45-minute slide-shows in a darkened room would come close.

There is, it must be said, the argument of whether a general company knowledge course is education or training. That is, does it make someone perform their job better, or is it merely creating an awareness? If it is training, then either format described above is most certainly wrong. If, on the other hand, it is education, then that is still no excuse for the way in which it is conducted.

Education, without retention of the knowledge imparted, is not education. As we saw earlier in this Chapter, we don't remember much of what we hear; we remember most by doing.

So, if an induction programme includes a session on credit control, what is wrong with bringing it to life by using participants as working displays? Objects (such as pens, models, and paper clips) can be placed on a table and each given a value. Participants are organized to represent buyers and suppliers. Transactions are arranged to take place, but money is not always handed over at the time of purchase.

Participants will be able to see what is happening, and soon some suppliers will be heavily out of pocket, while the buyers will realize their good fortune. The essence of credit control can be conveyed and the involvement can be continued using money tokens and the documentation and practices employed by the company. More is likely to be remembered – if not for the originality alone.

The Trainer/Designer

Perhaps the heading should read the designer trainer. For we should audit the competence of the trainer to fulfil identified needs, and to match the desired image of training within the company. Talking of competences, the Training and Development Lead Body (TDLB) has developed standards of competence for the training profession. These are called occupational standards.

First, the TDLB has defined the key purpose of the training profession; then it has devolved it into areas of purpose; then key roles; still further into elements; and finally into performance criteria with range indicators. It is proposed that the elements can be grouped in a variety of ways to meet the needs of a wide range of trainer roles, and these groups will become the units of competence for assessment. Current exploratory work also includes expansion of range indicators into range statements, and this should be completed by the end of 1991.

The principle behind these occupational standards is not dissimilar to the setting of training objectives, which we looked at earlier in this Chapter.

Where we had a collection of training objectives grouped under one aim, and that under a course or solution title, a similar hierarchy operates here. The performance criteria have the status of the training objectives; these 'standards' are then grouped under an element, equivalent to an aim; for course or solution title, the term 'unit of competence' is used, and there may be several elements in one unit in the way that there are several aims in one course. That course could fit into a programme of courses, the equivalent of which would be the key role.

Such an approach, with units of competence, makes it possible to form the basis of an accreditation scheme. This will allow evidence to be gathered on achievement of standards, which can then be submitted via a workplace assessor to the appropriate awarding body. When the individual being assessed meets the standards of performance set out by the National Council for Vocational Qualifications (NCVQ), he or she will be accredited with relevant units of a National Vocational Qualification (NVQ).

As far as the design of training solutions is concerned, the TDLB has identified as area B, to 'design training and development strategies and plans'. One of the key roles deriving from this is B2, which is to 'provide learning opportunities and support to enable individuals and groups to achieve their objectives.'

It is key role B2 which is the relevant one for training-designers to attain. Table 5.3 shows how this is devolved into suggested units of competence, with unit B22 being broken down further to show the appropriate elements.

Table 5.3 *Key role B2 (TDLB Standards)*

Key Role B2
Design strategies to assist individuals and groups achieve their objectives
    Suggested Unit of Competence B21
    Identify and agree training and development strategies that meet learning needs
    Suggested Unit of Competence B22
    Design learning programmes which meet learning needs
        Element B221
        Select and specify training and development processes
        Element B222
        Define and agree learning programme elements
        Element B223
        Specify processes and methods for evaluating progress towards objectives
        Element B224
        Specify strategies for evaluating learning programmes
Suggested Unit of Competence B23
Specify the resources needed to deliver programmes
Suggested Unit of Competence B24
Test, adapt and agree learning programme designs
Suggested Unit of Competence B25
Agree learning plans to deliver individuals' and groups' objectives

---

All of this is leading to a quality control mechanism for each vocational area. Where the trainer has been accredited with units of a National Vocational Qualification (NVQ), it is a signal to the training auditor that '*good* practice' is in place for those units of competence.

However, it may not mean that '*best* practice' is in place, nor may it mean that without the NVQ practice is poor; it could be that assessment just hasn't been carried out. There is still a role for the training auditor to play, but at least it makes the task easier.

Case Study: A Question of Need

The following demonstrates an organization with good intentions, whose expressed training need was not the root of the problem. It is recounted to show how important it is to identify real needs, before then exploring solutions with an open mind.

A major supplier of manned guarding services wanted to enhance its position in the market place. To achieve this, it sought to improve the conversion rate of presentations into new business, or at least into good prospects.

The Commercial Director obtained a brochure at a Business to Business exhibition, and rang to see if a training consultant could provide a one-day course in presentation skills for 15 of their managers. Fortunately, they allowed the consultant the opportunity of meeting them to discuss the requirement before any solution was proposed.

At that meeting it was important to find out:

1. Why had the need come about?
   – what was symptomatic of poor presentation skills?
2. What was the nature of the presentations and the objectives of each?
3. What previous training had the managers received, or what else was planned?
4. Why 15 people in one day?
5. How would they measure the effectiveness of the training?

Having listened both to the Commercial Director and the Operations Director, the consultant asked if it were possible to speak to some of these managers in order to understand their concerns.

In just two-and-a-half hours of discussions, and a tour of their Operations Centre, the real cause of the problem was all too obvious – to an outsider at least! It wasn't that they were lacking in presentation skills – they were lacking in selling skills. As in many organizations, the managers were such because of their technical or man-management experience. Yet they were expected to be front-line salesmen too.

This story confirms, above all, that one of the unspoken attributes of a trainer (and training auditor) is the ability to put yourself in other people's shoes. As company employees, the managers were so focused on meeting internal needs, and on the facilities which the company had, that they were unable to see the service from the customer's standpoint.

The consultant received the same guided tour and company presentation that 'Prospects' were given. He put himself in the shoes of a 'Prospect'. He therefore wanted to know what he might be buying.

The Commercial Director was a little taken aback, when in response to one of his tour statements, pointing out a particular feature of the Control Room, the consultant replied, 'So what?!' It was a question that had silently occurred on several previous occasions during his visit, but he could no longer contain it. The trouble was, many of their previous prospects obviously had.

The consultant explained. For most of the time there, a catalogue of features of the company had been revealed to him, but at no time were they accompanied by something akin to: ' . . . which means for Mr Prospect that . . . ' It was all tell and not sell.

With all credit to the Commercial Director and his colleagues, they, too, were prepared to listen and learn. What had set out as a request for 15 managers to be trained in one day in presentation skills, turned out to be:

1. An initial three days sales training course for one group of eight, and one of seven managers each.
   This incorporated:
   – Defining what the company had to offer.
   – Converting features to benefits (that the customer actually buys).
   – Selling against competition.
   – Overcoming objections
   – Making group presentations.
2. Follow-up events for each group for one day per month for six months. This also led to training in:
   – How to make appointments by telephone.
   – How to conduct hospitality events.
   – Controlling business phone calls.

The company also took on a new member of staff to continue this training in-house, and identify and satisfy all future training needs.

The company ought to be commended for allowing their perception of the root cause of the problem to be questioned, and for implementing such a radical change to their original plans for the betterment of the company.

Unfortunately, as a footnote, the two training companies who were also asked to tender for the assignment should be chastised for proposing how they would train the 15 managers in presentation skills in just one day!

► QUESTIONS FOR THE TRAINING AUDITOR ◄

- Are training needs clearly and correctly translated into training objectives?
- Is there a gap between what training solutions achieve and the training needs that were identified?

- Is every training solution thoroughly documented?
- Does each training solution have the right balance of economy, efficiency and frequency, or is there a predominant factor which affects effectiveness?

- What is the motivation behind the methodology of each solution?
- Does the methodology suit the training objectives?

- Is the Learning Agreement (or equivalent) available and being used throughout the company?

- Do managers present any resistance to staff applying what they have learned?

- Is there evidence that training plans are being implemented?

- Are all trainers accredited by the National Council for Vocational Qualifications for relevant units of competence?

6 Auditing the Validation and Evaluation Process

▷   SUMMARY   ◁

- Defines validation and evaluation. They are shown to be steps worth investigating within the training audit, although they do not themselves constitute an audit.
- Discusses appropriate validation techniques before reviewing what we might want evaluation to reflect. Some notes of caution are offered on the dangers of looking at results in absolute, rather than relative, terms.
- Provides a sample of occupational performance standards for the process of validation and evaluation – but has the Training and Development Lead Body got it right?
- The case study completing the Chapter indicates the pitfalls when validation takes place only after the solution has been implemented; and when the measure of evaluation is considered with total disregard for the effectiveness of training.

The Systems Approach

When defining what a training audit is, in Chapter 2, we reviewed those training activities which have often been confused with the term; among them is the process of validation and evaluation.

The Training and Development Lead Body has also set occupational standards for carrying out this process, as we shall see. Yet those standards do not tell us 'how' to go about the task of validating and evaluating, so much as the extent to which the task is carried out.

In Chapter 1, the National Audit Office Report identified that fewer than a quarter of the private sector companies reviewed had full and systematic methods of evaluation. Most did not have complete information on their training expenditure, while in the Civil Service, many training branches did not use the Measuring Training Activity system defined for the purpose of validation and evaluation. What evaluation did take place, of the benefits of training, was at an early stage.

So what is validation and evaluation, and how and when should it happen? The Department of Employment, in its *Glossary of Training Terms* in 1978, defined validation and evaluation of training as follows:

Validation
(a) External

A series of tests and assessments designed to ascertain whether the behavioural objectives of an internally valid training programme were realistically based on an accurate initial identification of training needs, in relation to the criteria of effectiveness adopted by the organization.

(b) Internal

A series of tests and assessments designed to ascertain whether a training programme has achieved the behavioural objectives specified.

Evaluation

The assessment of the total value of a training session in social as well as financial terms. The term is also used in the general judgemental sense of the continuous monitoring of a programme or of the training function as a whole.

Evaluation, therefore, differs from validation in that it attempts to measure the overall cost-benefit of the course or programme and not the achievement of its laid-down objectives. In fact, objectives are not as important to evaluation; evaluation is more concerned with measuring the changes brought about by training and, where possible, comparing them with what would have happened if the training had not taken place.

The terms of validation and evaluation are more usually used together, but they are different. It may still be appropriate, however, to refer to them as one process because validation is a step which leads directly into evaluation.

From those definitions, though, we can see that neither is examining the actual way the system works, and whether it represents 'best practice'. As we saw in Chapter 2; it is a step within the system itself and is, therefore, subject to the scrutiny of a training audit. Evaluation, for example, will tell you what a particular car is worth to you but not whether you could get a better one elsewhere. Let us take a look at validation first.

Validation

We have already seen that there are internal factors and external ones. Some mention has already been made in Chapter 5 of the need to check that a training solution has worked. This is done by taking the training objectives expressed *in* a solution and measuring the trainee's performance against those objectives. We are therefore examining boasts within, or internal to, the solution.

It may well be, then, that such internal boasts are valid, and that the trainee is now capable of doing whatever the training said he or she would be able to do.

External Validation

However, outside the solution itself – or external to it – we may discover that the need for the individual to undergo the training was not valid. This could be for one of two reasons:

Either:
There is no requirement within that individual's current or planned future job to have the skill, knowledge or attitude which the training addressed.
or:
The individual was already capable of doing what the training set out to achieve.

Looking at those two statements it may be apparent that we are trying to lock the stable door after the horse has bolted. As validation always seems to be the step immediately after the implementation of the solution, that is also when external validation usually takes place. Why?

If we apply the practices related in Chapter 4, then there should almost be no need for external validation. We could be accused of locking the stable door after the horse has already bolted it!

External validation has some value though, at the identification-of-needs stage, as a policing exercise to ensure that 'best practice' is being implemented.

Now, I can almost hear readers saying to themselves: 'He's conceded that validation is the same as doing an audit.' To put that thought to rest, validation is only 'what' we are doing, not 'how' we are doing it.

The training audit will tell us whether the way we validate conforms to 'best practice' or not. So if all the guidelines concerning the identification of training needs, offered in Chapter 4, are applied, then this amounts to 'best practice' for external validation.

Internal Validation

Internal validation can only take place during or after the training. By designing a solution around the considerations given in Chapter 5, we may be significantly increasing its chances of success. Yet, we also saw how an identical solution may work for one trainee but not for another.

So, how do we go about internal validation? Is it just straightforward testing of the trainee? Strictly speaking, the purpose of internal validation is to assess the effectiveness of the training, not to test the trainee. However, we cannot really do the former without having done the latter.

The method of assessing the trainee's post-training performance could be selected to suit the objectives of the training. Methods may include:

practical tests	quizzes
written tests	questionnaires
oral tests	on-job
projects	observation

Each has certain advantages or disadvantages, so suitability to the training objectives is the real key. For example, if a salesperson has undergone a one-week's training course in closing the sale, it may not prove a true validation simply to give him or her a written test afterwards. We would want to see evidence of the techniques being applied in immediate response to dialogue with a role-playing 'Prospect'.

When to use which method:

Practical tests
Where the outcome of the training is something practical, like displaying a skill or technique or following a procedure.

Applies generally to telephone techniques, interpersonal skills (including selling, presenting, interviewing and aspects of man-management) and machine operation. It can still provide a basis for learning from feedback, as doer or observer.

Written tests
Where retention of knowledge, rather than specific applications of it, is the desired outcome of training.

Not to be used if skills are being assessed. Learning can no longer be shared during testing, and results can be kept private between the trainee and the assessor. Perhaps, though, the job doesn't require levels of literacy.

Oral tests

These can vary in validity, according to whether or not all trainees have to answer the same questions and whether other trainees are present or not.

Where other trainees are present it is unlikely all will be asked the same questions, but at least learning can still continue if the answers are provided for each question.

These may differ from written tests in that here a quicker response time may be required for each question. Particularly valuable where speed of thought is needed.

Projects

Whereas practical tests tend to seek demonstration of the set methods, projects may allow more flexibility for the trainee. The project is as much a learning tool as it is a form of assessment.

Where self-motivation, self-discipline and initiative are being tested, this is the appropriate method to use.

However, it is sometimes difficult to distinguish results between inadequate guidance and training, or inadequacies of the trainee.

Quizzes

These are like an oral test in which not everyone gets the same questions, and answers are provided along the way.

Usually done in teams, they take the attention of individual trainees and can be viewed by them as fun, as well as a continuation of the learning process.

More useful where knowledge has to be applied (such as hypothetical situations), than just learning 'parrot fashion'.

Questionnaires

Unlike written tests, the term questionnaire usually refers to an 'opinionnaire' in which the trainees give their view of what they have learned, or haven't learned.

These have little value where validation is sought because they are only evidence of the trainees' perception of learning rather than of actual learning that has taken place; but they may contribute towards evaluation. The negative comments would generate cause for concern but the positive ones may not prove very much.

On-job observation

This is by far the most telling of all assessment methods. After all, the outcome of the training is to enhance performance in the job, not performance in tests.

The validation can only happen away from exam conditions, unless they exist in the trainee's job. An awareness of being assessed can make trainees concentrate more and perform better: on the other hand, there would be just as many who would wilt under such pressure and perform well below their usual standard.

Hence, an aggregate of test results from the same solution would give us a clearer indication of what hit and what missed; but perhaps we need one method of assessment to validate another. In which case, any of the first five could be used for immediate assessment at the end of the training (or during it, where practicals, projects and quizzes apply), with on-job observation being used more covertly.

Remember the Learning Agreement? That can be used to bring the manager and trainee together to discuss the training from both viewpoints. Any difficulties can then be brought out into the open and further action agreed upon, where necessary. Where a significant proportion of trainees all display the same difficulties, despite the training, then the solution itself will be called into question.

Therefore, there needs to be a system for gathering the relevant section of all Learning Agreements so that such trends could be identified and corrective action taken.

Training Co-ordinators

Training, as we have seen, is a function which must operate for the benefit of the company as a whole, and not just for isolated pockets of activity within the company. One or two training professionals cannot be in all places at once: but training itself can be.

I am very much an advocate of an in-company network of training co-ordinators; virtually a 'must' in large corporations. It need not be a full-time role, though it must require commitment and a fair amount of administrative skills from the job-holder.

This activity should be regarded not as a chore but as an important foothold on the ladder of management. It can complement the roles of some supervisors, would-be supervisors, or first-line management. It can even be fulfilled through job-rotation on a six-monthly or annual basis, to coincide with the company's training year.

The role of the training co-ordinator in each section, division or department, is to:

- Collate the training needs and forward them to the central training function (ctf), retaining a copy.
- Receive joining instructions for trainees from ctf, log them and distribute them.
- Chase up post-course assessments (such as the Learning Agreement), retain copies and forward them to ctf.
- Maintain training records of both off-job and on-job training.
- Provide the administrative and advisory link generally between their section, department, or division, and the central training function.

The role is not intended to divest line-management of its responsibilities towards training (see Chapter 4), but merely to take away some of the burden of administration and documentation that 'best practice' requires.

Further, such a network can reinforce the company's commitment to training and generate a more positive attitude towards it. Some co-ordinators may even come up with some good ideas to help the system, which should then be shared with the network.

Evaluation

The trainee represents the single biggest variable of any training activity. Solutions may be identical but trainees rarely are. Where validation tests the trainee, we have an assessment of the trainee (subject to comments made earlier in the Chapter): but where it tests the trainee in order to test the solution, we must be able to distinguish between achievement of objectives and the trainee's perceived value of the training received.

The latter is a case of evaluation rather than validation, and the two do not always marry. In a programme of 10 trainees, it may not be too surprising for the post-course assessment forms to indicate that either 10 different programmes were needed, or, in fact, that 10 different programmes took place!

At least it wouldn't be surprising if the training were conducted on the hit and miss, or mystery tour approach. That is to say that trainees did not know why they were on the programme and were left to decide at the end what they thought of it.

Where such discrepancies in feedback have occurred in the past, the finger of blame has pointed to either:

- poor solution design,

or

- incorrect identification of needs and participants, and therefore of training objectives.

Rarely ever did it point to no communication between manager and trainee in preparation for the training. So it would seem to have been doing the job of validation.

Also, the assessment forms (or 'happy sheets' as they are often called) do not always elicit complete and honest views when administered and collected by the trainer at the end of the training, just as participants want to go home.

The process can be enhanced, however, by improving the design of the assessment forms. Most training departments administer forms, but they tend to be the same generalist form even for different courses. It would be more effective if each course had a tailored assessment form which draws attention to the achievement of the particular course objectives, and to the application of specific learning points – in addition to the generalist questions about the training provider or methodology, and the course administration. Table 6.1 shows how an assessment form can be tailored to a particular course, in this case for telephone techniques training.

The form should at least address the same issues as a Learning Agreement (discussed in Chapter 5, see Figure 5.1) but, unlike the Learning Agreement which is eventually to be filed along with the trainee's personal record, the assessment form will be filed according to the course. This is so that changes can be made to the course if necessary. In other words, the Learning Agreement looks more at the individual or trainee while the assessment form reviews the course.

Working on the premise that best practice is being employed in identifying and documenting training needs, what would be the point of evaluation? If the need has been proven against company objectives, then surely it has value to the company. Does it therefore need putting into financial terms?

Table 6.1 *Telephone Techniques course assessment form*

COURSE ASSESSMENT
TELEPHONE TECHNIQUES

Name: Date:

1. **COURSE OBJECTIVES**

   To what extent were the following course objectives achieved for you? (please circle the appropriate number on the scale below):

   (a) To list the major differences between face-to-face and telephone communication.

       Not at all   1   2   3   4   Achieved completely

   (b) To handle complaints or aggressive callers without creating further antagonism, but by gaining their confidence.

       Not at all   1   2   3   4   Achieved completely

   (c) To recognize the different personality types encountered on the phone and demonstrate how to deal effectively with them.

       Not at all   1   2   3   4   Achieved completely

   (d) To list eight key points for making effective use of the telephone and apply these as a guideline for each call.

       Not at all   1   2   3   4   Achieved completely

   (e) To elicit the understanding of the other party without insulting them, so that the message is agreed by both parties.

       Not at all   1   2   3   4   Achieved completely

2. **APPLICATION**

   (a) To what extent do you feel you will be able to apply learning from this course to your work?

       Not at all   1   2   3   4   Completely

   (b) What were the most useful learning points that you can apply?

   (c) What were the least useful sessions? Why?

3. **TRAINING METHOD**

   (a) What comments do you have regarding the training methods used and the course material provided?

   (b) Did the trainer display any understanding of your work and relate the learning to your needs?

       Not at all   1   2   3   4   Completely

   Please support your answer with examples:

   (c) What changes, if any, would you make to the course?

The answer should be yes, if it can be done. Certainly, any expenditure on training should be recorded, as discussed in the previous chapter under economy. Instead of calling it expenditure, we call it investment – which is, after all, what it is. With any investment though, we need to determine the return on it. So what returns could we be looking for?

Returns on investment

We saw in Chapter 1 that it is not always possible to put up true cash values on the outcome of training, and that rather than a cost-benefit analysis we are aiming at a measure of cost-effectiveness.

Cost, though, should only become a feature of the measure when effectiveness is established. That is, only when the process of validation has shown that the training activity of the company is helping the company meet all its training needs, thereby enabling it to meet company objectives. At that point you can calculate the expenditure on training and assess whether the same results could have been achieved more cheaply, or whether even more results could have been achieved at the same cost. This, however, becomes a measure of economy rather than an evaluation.

Where effectiveness of training is not evident, the expenditure (or economy) could still be calculated, but it would seem wrong to call it cost-effectiveness.

So what sort of changes could be observed that would indicate a social or financial value of training to the company? After all, the essence of evaluation is in comparisons. We could, perhaps, look for measures in the areas shown in Table 6.2.

(a) Average number of training days per person.
(b) Amount of training by activity or department.
(c) Proportional impact on profits.
(d) Improved job performance.
(e) Impact on staff retention.
(f) Degrees of proactive versus reactive training
(g) Reductions in complaints, jobs re-done or wastage of materials.
(h) Scope of training professionalism provided.

Table 6.2 *Areas to be evaluated*

The average number of training days per person is a measure which has often been used as a basis for comparisons. These can be made between one year and another, or between companies of a similar size or business. While it is a quantitative factor, the quality lies in the quality of the company's objectives, which are being supported by the training.

The measure could indicate the productivity rate of training, or help us arrive at the average investment cost of training per head. However, it focuses on training itself and not on the impact of training.

Such information may have more value when linked to specific activities or departments, rather than when just seen in absolute terms.

The amount of training by activity or department can reveal a lot more to us about company attitudes towards training. Perhaps training is always effective in that needs are always being met – but are priorities also being met?

If we observe that the training function is occupied only in maintenance tasks or reactive tasks, then we could conclude that the company is doing its best to keep up with yesterday. Perhaps the money could be better spent preparing it to meet tomorrow's needs; or maybe more money should be invested.

It could be that some departments are getting significantly more attention than others. Is this because:

- They are better organized?
- Their needs take priority?
- There are significantly more people?
- There is a higher proportion of less experienced staff?
- There is a higher turnover of staff?
- The trainer knows that department's activities better than those of other departments?
- Other departments' managers are not disposed to the role of training?

In a year when management has had a high profile, was it at the expense of fundamental job skills, leaving behind a waiting list of the needy? Where specific activities had such attention, was there a noticeable impact on performance or profits which were wholly attributable to it?

Hence the points (c) to (h) in Table 6.2 are more to do with impacts than with the numbers game. Even the scope of training expertise available is a result of the investment in training. Are the trainers themselves meeting their own needs and developing the training function to cope with the company's anticipated demands?

The most difficult aspect of evaluation is trying to isolate training as the cause of the change, when other factors could have played a significant role too. While it is not a precise science, evaluation will still provide information. Precision is supplied by every other stage of the systematic approach to training, because there are objectives against which we can measure performance. The training auditor, though, should look at the systems used for evaluation to ensure that the extent of the impacts (observed changes) would not have occurred if the training had not taken place.

Another way of distinguishing between validation and evaluation is that the former tells us more about the supply of training, while the latter considers demand implications more fully.

Evaluation is really saying: 'What do we expect to get back from our investment in training? Are we solely hoping to achieve an average of four training days per person per year – while striving towards company objectives – or are we striving to improve profits by enhancing the effectiveness of individuals?' Evaluation therefore provides the justification for training. At the end of the day, it should show that the Training Department is fulfilling the promise it gave when publishing its training policy.

The training audit, in contrast, examines the systematic approach to validation and evaluation, and the effect of findings on other stages of the training process, which we identified in Chapter 2, Figure 2.2. It determines the value for money rather than the justification of training.

Occupational Performance Standards

The Training and Development Lead Body (TDLB) has identified as area of purpose D, 'the process of evaluating the effectiveness of training and development'. Table 6.3 shows how this is broken down into key roles D1, D2 and D3.

Also shown are the suggested units of competence applicable to D1, as they closely resemble the discussion of evaluation in this Chapter. These are devolved into elements by the TDLB, which can be enhanced in-company.

However, when looking at key role D2, you will notice that it is to 'evaluate individual and group achievements against objectives'. The suggested units of competence below it (D21, D22 and D23) give us a better clue to what is required. May I offer a word of caution? Where it says 'evaluate' please read 'validate'!

Area D   Evaluate the effectiveness of training and development
Key Role D1
Evaluate the effectiveness of training and development
> *Suggested Unit of Competence D11*
> Plan and set up systems for evaluating the training and development function
> *Suggested Unit of Competence D12*
> Evaluate the training and development function
> *Suggested Unit of Competence D13*
> Modify systems and practices to improve training and development

Key Role D2
Evaluate individual and group achievements against objectives
> *Suggested Unit of Competence D21*
> Plan and set up systems to evaluate the achievement of objectives
> *Suggested Unit of Competence D22*
> Evaluate the achievement of outcomes against learning objectives
> *Suggested Unit of Competence D23*
> Modify and adapt learning plans

Table 6.3   *Area D (TDLB Standards)*

The training profession ought to sort out its terminology and here is a good place to start. We know now what a training audit is, and what it is not, so we may as well be clear as to what validation is, and evaluation is not! It is hoped that the Training and Development Lead Body will soon resolve the confusion in its published standards.

Case Study: In the Distant Past

Several years ago now, an insurance group operating in the UK provided clients with product knowledge and sales training, relating to creditor insurance products.

As far as evaluation went, it was seen as simple by the client: training had done its job when product penetration reached 40 per cent. So, if it didn't reach the target set, training had failed.

However, even though consultants were there to advise or recommend, after careful listening, the decision about the solution was still the client's. In many cases, where money was the primary object of introducing the creditor (or consumer credit) insurance product anyway, economy was the deciding factor. In the case of clients with a network of branches, their view was often that it would be less costly to have the consultant train the branch managers, rather than have the consultant go to all the branches. The managers could then carry out the training at their branch. That was not the only way to save money for, in addition, the branch managers were only spared for a half-day.

The less rewarding side of training is when you are put in the situation of going through the motions, and you know that achieving the objectives will be more by luck than judgement. Well, once or twice you could be lucky, but evidence shows that luck never lasts for long. For, although the clients could evaluate training in their terms, they were often blind to the validation aspects and the factors which gave rise to the effectiveness of training.

What was wrong, then, with spending a half-day training the branch managers? Most consultants will favour the training of trainers and promoting self-help, but only in the right conditions. It should be pointed out that in the majority of cases:

- The branch managers were responsible for training, but were not trained in training or coaching techniques.
- They, too, were completely new to the creditor insurance product.
- They were of differing abilities.
- Some branches were bigger than others.
- Their motivation for selling the product was different from that of branch staff.
- They felt that authority was on their side.
- They had other duties and responsibilities too.

In a half-day training programme, it was possible to validate the knowledge of a group of 10 branch managers, but not to test them as individuals. There was little or no time to see that knowledge applied in selling situations.

Further, there was no validation of their ability to train staff at the branches. Would they all put the information across as it should be done? Would they all even put it across in the same way? Would they find time for role-playing in the session? Where the client's branches were retail stores, how would the branch manager cope with training new sales assistants as a result of staff turnover?

Obviously, distance-learning materials could be developed, but they cost money. Sometimes, the initial training did reap rewards close to 40 per cent product penetration, but failure to maintain the training led to typical penetrations of only 15–20 per cent within one to two years.

Perhaps the 40 per cent could even have been 80 per cent, if a more effective system of validation had been set up.

Remember, validation should present an immediate measure of success or failure, such as whether trainees display a thorough knowledge of the product and demonstrate how to apply it in selling situations. Product penetration of 40 per cent is more global and longer term, and is an evaluation of what the training should achieve.

Validation is also about establishing whether the needs were correctly set in the first place. In one particular assignment of creditor insurance training, the identification of product knowledge and related selling skills as inadequate and in need of attention, proved not to be the cause of low product penetration. Moreover, the bulk of the 'targeted' audience were not those with the need anyway.

Having been reassured by the client of answers to certain questions, it became evident during the second of 20 planned half-day training sessions that the solution to selling more of the product did not really rest in the training being provided.

The showrooms in question usually had specialist Finance and Insurance (F&I) managers who had a number of finance and related creditor insurance products at their disposal. There was always an F&I manager at the bigger showrooms, where there were also more sales staff. Yet, the training was aimed at the sales staff who did not sell the finance – they only sold the showroom goods before passing the customer on to the F&I manager to deal with the financial aspects.

It was then discovered that the competitor products were either quicker to confirm acceptance of customers for loans, or had insurance benefits for the showroom customers which the customers specifically asked for.

These problems were not insurmountable, but much time, effort and cost was misdirected through lack of validation. All it needed was a bit of two-way communication – if the sales staff and F&I managers had been consulted in the first place, the proper solutions would have been found earlier.

Unfortunately, this experience is representative of many training programmes which are born out of management's assumptions. One wonders, perhaps, if distance-learning was a term brought about by distance-management.

► QUESTIONS FOR THE TRAINING AUDITOR ◄

- Do managers recognize the distinction between validation and evaluation?
- Is there evidence that the two are confused?

- What steps are taken to validate each training solution?
- Is each step appropriate to the objectives of the training?
- How is the information from validation fed back into the system for the re-designing of solutions or re-assessment of needs?

- How are the benefits of each solution evaluated – is it short-term or long-term?

- What changes are observed which provide an evaluation of the training function?

- What documentation is completed within the process of validation and evaluation?

- Does the training function fulfil its statement of intent given in the training policy statement?
- Are the trainers accredited by the National Council for Vocational Qualifications for relevant units of competence?

Epilogue

So there were three managers in the managing director's office. Two of them had already had their say in justifying their existence over redundancy. Now it was the turn of the training manager. What could he say?

'Well,' he began, 'I am delighted that my fellow managers are so successful in contributing profit to the company we all support. It makes my hard work so much more worthwhile.'

The choking of one manager was almost smothered by the demands of the MD to be told more.

'You see,' he continued, 'the new standards of efficiency established by the production department were achieved through a programme of retraining. In consultation with the production manager and union representative, I designed a strategy for retraining operatives in the skills demanded of the new production line.'

The MD looked across to the production manager who nodded assent.

'I have also ensured that standards can be maintained even with employee changes on the line. All the supervisors are trained in on-job coaching skills now, which has given them greater job satisfaction and allows training of new people in the department to start immediately, without any significant loss of production.'

The marketing manager knows what is coming next.

'The return on marketing is made all the more profitable thanks to the help of a consultant working closely with the marketing manager. The right consultant for the job was identified by me in response to a request from the marketing manager. That same consultant and I are now designing a distance-learning package, so that the knowledge required to make our marketing so profitable can be shared with future managers of the department.'

The MD's eyes dilate as the more than usual amount of light passes through them.

'Am I to conclude,' he begins to ask, as though knowing the answer already, 'that you can take someone else's objective and devise a strategy to help them achieve it?'

The training manager was about to give the answer, which wasn't needed, when the MD enthused:

'In our current climate, there will be a reassessment of many objectives throughout the company, many of which have not been achieved before. I can see that some retraining will be appropriate, but I will need to use strategies that are not costly and which give us value for money. I shall require your professional expertise more than ever.'

The MD motions the three managers towards the door with his thanks, as he contemplates the hope that lies ahead.

He is about to sit down again when he calls out for the training manager. 'You left your book by your chair . . .' he says. '. . . *How to Take a Training Audit.*'

'I've read it,' came an assured and confident reply, 'but I would like it returned when you've finished reading it too!'

Appendix: Training Audit Rating Guide

▷ SUMMARY OF THE TRAINING AUDIT PROCESS ◁

- The training auditor should be comparing current practice to best practice. He or she should not only find out about the present situation, but should look for future trends.
- The auditor is looking for evidence of a system, and can do this by examining the four stages of the Training Audit Loop:

    1. The company objectives and training policy.
    2. Identification of training needs.
    3. The training solutions.
    4. Validation and evaluation.

- The best system is one which not only enables value for money to be assessed, but which can sustain itself throughout changes in management. Systems procedures must be clearly identified and available, as must documentation which must also be implemented properly.
- To test the system thoroughly, the training auditor should not only review the effectiveness of documentation and procedures, but should also interview management and employees to see if the system is working for them.
- Such an audit cannot be conducted in one day, nor perhaps in one week; it must be thorough if it is to have any value at all. We don't want a situation of the kettle calling the pot black!
- Use the following rating guide to assess the value for money of training in your company.

Training Audit Rating Guide

Rating	Findings
G	Training takes place on a haphazard basis, without any central co-ordination, plans or system documentation. Needs are not related to objectives.
F	Some departments have their own form of training plans, but still no system documentation or identification of needs.
F+	As for F, but with the addition that training records are maintained to show the plan is carried out.
E	All departments have a one-year training plan which is consistent with company style.
E+	As for E, but with supporting evidence that the plan is implemented.
D	All employees are considered within the implemented department training plans and at least one method of identifying training needs is used.
C	Documentation partially exists for co-ordinating training centrally and training solutions are validated against needs.
B-	All needs are based on performance standards against company objectives. Thorough documentation is used to enable evaluation of the results of training.
B	A long-term training plan, for five years, is in operation throughout the company, in addition to the above.
A	The company is awarded ISO 9001 (BS 5750 or EN 29001) status and the training system is maintained accordingly; *and/or* The company operates an accreditation scheme of competence-based performance standards, complete with training system documentation; *and/or* The trainers are accredited by the National Council for Vocational Qualifications for relevant units of competence.
A+	As for A, with the addition of the company managers having been awarded unit of competence I5 from the Management Charter Initiative, and/or A2 from the occupational standards for the training profession.
A++	As for A+, but everything has been in place for at least three years, system documentation records improvements in performance standards, and the benefits of training are constantly evident.

Select Bibliography

British Standards Institute (1987), *Quality Assurance: BSI Handbook 22*, BSI.

Buckley, R and Caple, J (1989), *The Theory and Practice of Training*, Kogan Page.

Department of Employment (1978), *Glossary of Training Terms*, HMSO.

Fletcher, Shirley (1991), *NVQs, Standards and Competence*, Kogan Page.

Haldane, Tom (1989), *Meeting Quality Standards*, Pergamon Open Learning.

Jackson, Terence (1989), *Evaluation: Relating Training to Business Performance*, Kogan Page.

National Audit Office, *A Framework for Value for Money Audits*, HMSO.

National Audit Office (1990), *Training of Non-Industrial Civil Servants*, HMSO.

Training and Development Lead Body (1991), *National Standards for Training & Development*, The Employment Department, Sheffield.

Index